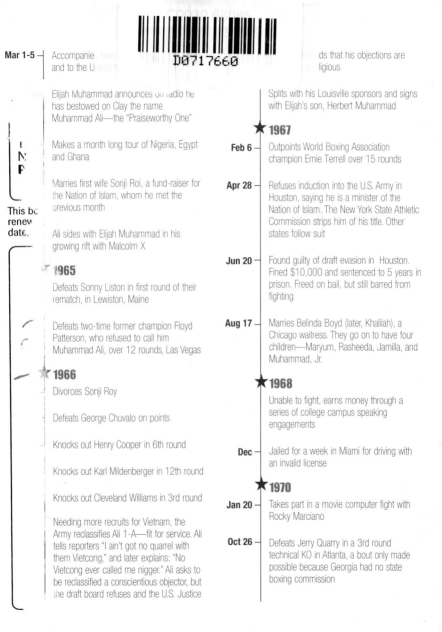

Mar 1-5 — Accompanie[...] [...]ds that his objections are
and to the U[...] [...]ligious

Elijah Muhammad announces on radio he
has bestowed on Clay the name
Muhammad Ali—the "Praiseworthy One"

Makes a month long tour of Nigeria, Egypt
and Ghana

Marries first wife Sonji Roi, a fund-raiser for
the Nation of Islam, whom he met the
previous month

Ali sides with Elijah Muhammad in his
growing rift with Malcolm X

★ 1965

Defeats Sonny Liston in first round of their
rematch, in Lewiston, Maine

Defeats two-time former champion Floyd
Patterson, who refused to call him
Muhammad Ali, over 12 rounds, Las Vegas

★ 1966

Divorces Sonji Roy

Defeats George Chuvalo on points

Knocks out Henry Cooper in 6th round

Knocks out Karl Mildenberger in 12th round

Knocks out Cleveland Williams in 3rd round

Needing more recruits for Vietnam, the
Army reclassifies Ali 1-A—fit for service. Ali
tells reporters "I ain't got no quarrel with
them Vietcong," and later explains: "No
Vietcong ever called me nigger." Ali asks to
be reclassified a conscientious objector, but
the draft board refuses and the U.S. Justice

Splits with his Louisville sponsors and signs
with Elijah's son, Herbert Muhammad

★ 1967

Feb 6 — Outpoints World Boxing Association
champion Ernie Terrell over 15 rounds

Apr 28 — Refuses induction into the U.S. Army in
Houston, saying he is a minister of the
Nation of Islam. The New York State Athletic
Commission strips him of his title. Other
states follow suit

Jun 20 — Found guilty of draft evasion in Houston.
Fined $10,000 and sentenced to 5 years in
prison. Freed on bail, but still barred from
fighting

Aug 17 — Marries Belinda Boyd (later, Khalilah), a
Chicago waitress. They go on to have four
children—Maryum, Rasheeda, Jamilla, and
Muhammad, Jr.

★ 1968

Unable to fight, earns money through a
series of college campus speaking
engagements

Dec — Jailed for a week in Miami for driving with
an invalid license

★ 1970

Jan 20 — Takes part in a movie computer fight with
Rocky Marciano

Oct 26 — Defeats Jerry Quarry in a 3rd round
technical KO in Atlanta, a bout only made
possible because Georgia had no state
boxing commission

Muhammad Ali
handbook

Muhammad Ali
handbook

Dave Zirin

M Q P
MQ Publications Ltd

ALI

Introduction

"Raid! Kills bugs dead!" That was the first message I ever heard from Muhammad Ali. The man who gave us unforgettable phrases like "float like a butterfly sting like a bee," "rumble young man rumble," "I ain't got no quarrel with them Vietcong" originally came to my attention on a TV ad. I asked my father who that funny man was and he told me simply, "That's the greatest."

It took two decades for me to connect the puffy-faced man who promoted a bug spray with Muhammad Ali in his full glory. I wanted to write about "The Greatest" because of how his image is being used now. William Faulkner once wrote, "The past isn't over. It's not even past." Ali's past has been edited and reedited almost beyond recognition. An Ali school of falsification has been running at full throttle since 1996. That year, the Champ, his hands trembling, his back stooped, lit the Olympic torch in front of a global audience. Never had the nakedness of disability been so candidly on display. Never had the oldest drama, that of the prodigal son returning "home" been so dramatically rendered. The connection between Ali and his audience crackled and sparked a renaissance of interest.

Sadly, the response to this revived fascination was a plethora of books and retrospectives swamped with obfuscation, spin, and slander. The dominant discourse runs through the "Sanitize Ali" movement. The

Page 2: **Courthouse, Houston, Texas, May 8, 1967**
Muhammad Ali kisses baby Claire Marie Woods while waiting to surrender himself to the court after refusing to accept induction into the U.S. Army.

Page 5: **State Opera, Vienna, November 19, 1999**
Ali, winner in the Contact Sports category, poses with his trophy at the World Sports Award of the Century Gala.

emissaries of this group present the Champ as a harmless symbol. He is now deemed safe for public appearances, Super Bowl commercials, and political photo ops. He can appear in ads to explain the war on terror to the Muslim world, as easily as he can shill for Microsoft. He can be fêted at the White House by George W. Bush.

The other approach comes from the "Smear Ali" crowd. This is represented by a new cottage industry of books that attempt to prove in the words of one that "Ali was an unapologetic sexist and unabashed racist" who "was bad for America." Both wings of the Ali School of Falsification share a common aim: the obliteration of who he was and the impact he had on those around him—not just friends and fans, but his incalculable effect on the social movements, emerging mass culture, and global media of his day. The young audiences who first encountered Ali's political comments were part of the most important struggles, both in the United States and around the world, since World War II. And that makes a full view of his life all the more important.

Ali's story could not be more relevant and the reclamation of his history—free of both opportunism and slander—could not be more pressing. We live in an era where sports has become an industry that towers titanically over the grandest dreams of its founders. It is bigger than U.S. steel, and counts its profits in the hundreds of billions. The stars of the sports world are given a platform that towers over other celebrities not to mention elected leaders. But all that comes at a price: it comes branded with corporate logos and the expectation that those given the platform will toe the line.

Muhammad Ali represents a different paradigm: he simply would not be who they wanted him to be. And we are richer not only for his experience but also his example.

Note: All quotations are from Muhammad Ali unless otherwise indicated

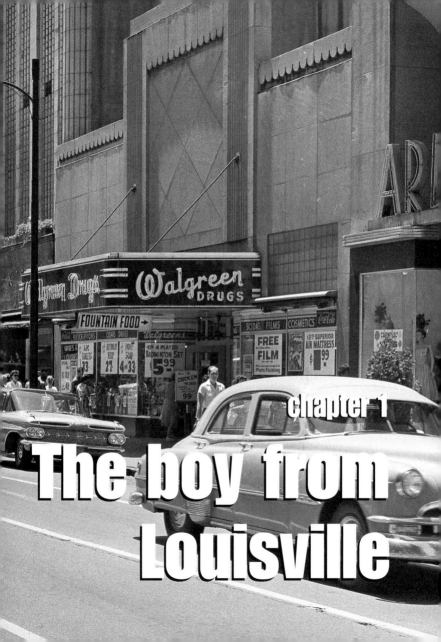

chapter 1

The boy from Louisville

Louisville childhood 1942–1960

Muhammad Ali was born Cassius Marcellus Clay in Louisville, Kentucky, to Cassius, Sr. and Odessa Clay on January 16th 1942. His birthday was only slightly over a month after the bombing of Pearl Harbor and the formal entrance of the United States in World War II.

Legal Jim Crow segregation ruled the south and *de facto* economic segregation the north. Despite the second-class citizenship offered African-Americans, they signed up to fight the "Good War" in great numbers. The contradictions were striking to both the soldiers abroad and their families at home. As one soldier recounted, "I was over there [in Europe] fightin' Hitler and all his hate, and my battalion was as segregated as a Dixie lunch counter."

The Louisville of Ali's youth embodied these contradictions. As writer Beverly Edwards said, "Kentucky is known as the Gateway to the South, but we weren't too much different from the Deep South as far as race was concerned." Louisville, home of bluegrass and the Kentucky Derby, was a deeply segregated, horse breeding community where the ceiling for Black ambition ended at preacher, school teacher, or stable-worker.

Previous page: **Louisville, Kentucky, July 3, 1959**
Near the corner of 4th and Walnut Streets. Walnut Street was renamed Muhammad Ali Boulevard in the 1970s to honor Louisville's famous son.
Right: **Louisville, Kentucky, 1954**
The 12-years old Cassius Marcellus Clay, Jr., is shown posing prior to his amateur ring debut, a three-minute, three-round split decision over another novice named Ronnie O'Keefe.

... **nothing could compare to the week of the Kentucky Derby, with Derby night the most important social holiday of the year ... the same people every year and always the best.**

Manager, Brown's Hotel, Louisvile

Left: **Churchill Downs, Louisville, Kentucky, May 3, 1952**
Jockey Eddie Arcaro is kissed by his mother after winning the Kentucky Derby. On the left is Lucille Parker Wright, racing stable owner and Ben Jones (second from left), horse trainer, members of Louisville's racing elite.

Home life

The Clay family was a pressure cooker of thwarted hopes. They were a working class family that owned their own home. As Mike Marqusee said in the documentary, "Muhammad Ali: Through the Eyes ofthe World":

It was something of a myth that Muhammad Ali came from a middle-class Black background. Muhammad Ali's background was just like that of hundreds of thousands of other people who were Black, working class Southerners.

Ali's roots are in the soil that nurtured the most explosive social movement of the last fifty years—the Black Freedom struggle of the 1950s and 60s. Ali's home life was directed by two very different parental personalities. They combined to raise a child who would become a study in beguiling contrasts: someone both aggressively loquacious, and strikingly gentle; someone who feared physicality and excelled at the most violent sport of them all; someone who struggled in school but talked circles around anyone in the room.

Having a stable two-parent home, with food on the table every night, practically makes the young Clay a Sultan by the standards of the families that produce championship boxers in the U.S. Boxing is the sport of the poor where hunger in the ring mirrors the actual hunger with which many fighters were raised.

As George Foreman, one of Ali's future opponents, said to me, "I was hungry most of the time. The only question I would ask myself about the world was 'How do I get something to eat?' I didn't love school because I wanted to disguise that I was poorer than everybody else … I didn't know anything about anything except being hungry."

The Clays never lacked for clothing on their back or food on the table. As Clay, Sr. said of his two sons, Cassius and Rudolph:

I dressed them up as good as I could afford. They didn't come out of no Ghetto. I raised them on the best street I could: 3302 Grand Avenue in the west end of Louisville.

But the home was not without discord, violence, and an atmosphere of acute frustration. Clay, Sr. found escape in the bottle and other women, but when he was lucid he was a known charmer, loquacious and sharp. He was also someone who spoke very highly of Marcus Garvey and Garvey's Black Nationalist Back to Africa campaign, which in the 1920s was the first mass movement of African-Americans in the United States. This atmosphere of alcohol, religion, thwarted talents and Garveyite longings shaped the young Cassius.

Cassius was also shaped by his mother, who was universally regarded as a kind soul. Classmate Janet Geurin remembered, "Clay, Sr. was a good-looking, dark brown skin, dashing kind of person. He probably got his styling and profiling from that. But I think the inner core of him is his mother."

A genetic splicing of the gentle and the brash was on display from birth. Cassius loved to talk a big game, but he abhorred sports where he could get hurt. His brother Rudolph said, "We'd play touch football in the street and it would be hard to tag him because of his speed. But tackle football he didn't like. He wouldn't play because he thought it too rough."

A twist of fate—the famous stolen bicycle

The story of how Cassius fell into boxing, that most brutal of sports, reads almost like a fairy tale conjured by a folklorist, or a sharpie in a Hollywood pitch meeting. But it's true. The young boy had stopped at the community center to get some ice cream only to find that his treasured Schwinn bicycle had been stolen under his nose.

He went on and on about how he was going to "whup" whoever stole his bike. A police officer named Joe Martin, who was also a boxing instructor, overheard him and said, "Well you better learn how to fight before you start challenging people that you're gonna whup." So Clay met his first trainer, a white policeman the others gibingly nicknamed "Sergeant" because he stayed on for decades, content never to take the Sergeant's exam. Six weeks later, the lanky 89-pounder won his first fight, over Ronnie O'Keefe.

Unlike some athletes whose genius is evident on first glance, Cassius was not an obvious choice as the next heavyweight champ. As Joe Martin remembered, "If boxers were paid money on potential like ballplayers are, I don't know if he would have received one. He stood out because I guess he had more determination than most boys and he had the speed to get him someplace. He was a kid willing to make the sacrifices necessary to achieve something worthwhile in sports. I realized it was almost impossible to discourage him. He was easily the hardest worker of any kid I taught."

This desire was evident to everyone who saw him fight. "Ali spent all his time in the gym," said fellow fighter Jimmy Ellis. "That's where he lived. He wanted to box and he wanted to be great. And that's what his life was all about. I never saw him fight in the streets. I never saw him pushing or shoving outside the ring. Even then he did a lot of talking, telling guys they couldn't beat him, saying he was going to knock everyone out."

Two aspects of Clay's future fighting persona showed themselves immediately, however—his penchant for keeping his hands low, and his whipsaw reflexes. Bob Surkeim, who refereed many of Clay's young fights said:

I saw him with his hands down, standing there looking like he was going to get bombed out, and all of a sudden realizing that God had given this kid reflexes like no one had ever seen."

Later Angelo Dundee, Clay's longtime trainer, would echo Surkeim's comments, famously uttering, "He destroyed a generation of fighters by boxing with his hands down. Everyone else who did that got creamed but Ali was so quick he could get away with it."

His mouth of course finally found a place to be heard. Fellow fighter, and future opponent, Ernie Terrell said, "He had the same big mouth he had when he turned pro." Even as a very young man he said to the papers, "This guy must be done. I'll stop him in one."

Clay's endless enthusiasm and dedication was spurred by his desire to rise above his circumstances. In 1959, he became the first fighter from Louisville to win a title in the Golden Gloves Tournament of Champions in Chicago. He also won the national Amateur Athletic Union light-heavyweight title—an accomplishment he would repeat the following year.

During this period, Clay first proclaimed himself "the Greatest." 1959 was also the year in which he first happened on an organization called the Nation of Islam. He was strongly attracted to their mix of pride, anger, and mythology.

Determined to succeed

Despite diving into the ring, Clay retained his gentle demeanor. He once turned down a friendly game saying, "I could get hurt playing football and that would be bad for my boxing."

But the basics of being Black in the south, haunted his upbringing. His brother remembered, "Growing up the only problems Muhammad and I had with whites were if we were in a certain part of town. If we were in the wrong place, white boys would come up to us and say, 'Hey nigger. What are you doing here?'" Ali used to say that from the age of ten he would think about racism, lie in his bed, and cry … "When I was growing up, too many colored people thought it was better to be white."

When I started boxing, all I really wanted was someday to buy my mother and father a house and own a nice big car for myself. I figured I could make four thousand dollars just for one night. Then my dreams started to grow … I started boxing because I thought this was the fastest way for a Black person to make it in this country.

Right: **Louisville, Kentucky, 1960**
Cassius Clay (right) and his brother, Rudy, fool around with a medicine ball during training.

The lynching of Emmett Till

The young Cassius Clay was greatly shaken by the brutal murder in 1955 of 14 year old Emmett Till. Till was savagely beaten and killed in Mississippi after being heard to be "fresh to a white woman." His killers were acquitted and his mother held an open casket funeral so the world could see what they had done to her son. Pictures of Till's beautiful, delicate face—a face eerily similar to that of a certain young man in Louisville—beaten and torn beyond recognition, was broadcast around the country. Cassius was thirteen when Till was murdered, and he would recall its effects on his psyche as he became older.

But at this point Cassius, despite his stunning verbosity, was not someone who could either easily articulate his feelings or even excel in school. Classmate Geurin recalled, "In school they never picked him as somebody who would make a change in the world. They just didn't. He wasn't a football player, he wasn't a basketball player … he would jog alongside the school bus and shout out your name, for God's sake he was a boxer! He was kind of a nerd."

But this "nerd" was starting to make a name for himself. He fought 108 fights, winning six Kentucky Golden Gloves, two National Golden Gloves, and two National AAU titles by the time he was eighteen. The media was starting to notice, and he began signing autographs, writing alongside his name, "The Greatest."

Left: **Undated press photo**
This photo shows Emmett Louis Till, a 14-year-old black boy from Chicago, who was tortured and killed for allegedly whistling at a white woman in 1955 while visiting relatives in Mississippi.

A turbulent father

Cassius Marcellus Clay, Sr. (who was named for the 19th century abolitionist and politician Cassius Clay) was a known charmer, a verbose ladies man who never let marriage get in the way of a good time. As David Remnick has written:

Clay Sr. was cock of the walk, a braggart, a charmer, a performer, a man full of fantastical tales and hundred-proof blather." Ali said to a reporter years later, "My Daddy is a playboy. He's always wearing white shoes, pink pants, and blue shirts and he says he'll never get old."

As his son became famous, Clay, Sr. showed where "Gaseous Cassius" got his "Louisville Lip." As reporters gathered at his modest home, Clay, Sr. was known to regale them with stories about his time as an Arabian sheik or a Hindu noble. But beneath the smooth talk, and velvet-tongued braggadocio, was a man who seethed with the frustrations of wasted talent.

Clay, Sr. was a sign painter with a ninth grade education who nonetheless was a prodigiously skilled self-taught artist. Despite having no formal training, he painted murals at churches and schools across the city. He was able to make a decent living, buying a modest house for $4,500 in Louisville's all Black West End. This was seen as a step up from Smoketown, known as "the dark side of town."

But the artist who used his paint for signs and brick walls instead of canvases brought his stifled ambitions home and the tensions between Ali's parents could be explosive. Police records show Clay, Sr. arrested on numerous occasions for public drunkenness and driving under the influence. On three separate instances, the police were called by Odessa to stop him from abusing her. As Robert Lipsyte has said, "His father was a violent man. I wouldn't be surprised if he in some way, perhaps only emotionally, terrorized Cassius and his brother."

A young friend was once quoted as saying:

It always seemed to me that Ali suffered a great psychological wound when he was a kid because of his father, and that as a result he really shut down … there is a lot of pain there, and though he's always tried to put it behind him, a lot of that pain comes from his father, the drinking, the occasional violence, the harangues.

Clay, Sr. was never shy about sharing his sense of being wronged at the dinner table. He spoke very highly of Marcus Garvey and Garvey's Black Nationalist Back to Africa campaign which in the 1920s was the first mass movement of African-Americans in the United States.

This atmosphere of alcohol, religion, thwarted talents and Garveyite longings shaped the young Ali. But while his father's gift of the gab was passed seamlessly to the young Ali, his rough edges and bouts of cruelty were not. This is because of the other parental influence in Ali's life, his mother Odessa.

I was born painting ... and if it wasn't for the way things were at the time, a lot more people would have known what I could do... I don't have a favorite painting I've done. To be honest, they're all good.

Cassius Clay, Sr.

Left: **Louisville, Kentucky, 1965**

Cassius was named after his father, Cassius M. Clay, Snr.

Marcus Garvey: his father's political hero

Many Blacks living in the southern states of the U.S.A. supported the doctrines of Jamaican-born Marcus Garvey. Like other proponents of Black Nationalism, he believed that there are no allies for Black Americans to be found in the conventional movements against racism. Rather, he sought to "unite all people of African ancestry of the world to one great body to establish a country and absolute government of their own."

The 1920s saw the spread of lynchings in the south and the rise of the Ku Klux Klan as a mass force. This is when Blacks witnessed the most dramatic impact of Marcus Garvey and his United Negro Improvement Association (UNIA). The organization had the passive and active following of more than a million African-Americans who stood by Garvey's calls for self-reliance, community control, and a return back to Africa.

The majority of Blacks had no real interest in going back to Africa, but they identified with the assertion of pride and a sense of community in a dehumanizing world. The fathers of both Malcolm X and Muhammad Ali were influenced greatly by Garvey's teachings. But Garvey's group withered during the Depression—at a time when multi-racial movements were making greater material gains for African-Americans than race-based politics.

Right: **Lennox Avenue, Harlem, New York City, August, 1922**
Cassius Clay, Snr. admired Black nationalist Marcus Garvey, who is seen here dressed in military uniform as the "Provisional President of Africa." This was a parade held to celebrate the opening day exercises of the annual Convention of the Negro Peoples of the World.

A gentle, loving mother

If Cassius Clay, Sr. was a flashy dresser, who could charm a room in public, and seethe in anger at home, his wife Odessa Grady Clay was his diametric opposite. Odessa was a happy, round-faced woman, universally regarded as kind and gentle to those around her. A classmate recalled that Cassius's mother "impressed me as gentle … I think that was the essence of him, what his mother instilled in him."

Odessa worked as a domestic to some of Louisville's wealthiest families. She would read scripture to her sons in their cribs, and even when later she was troubled by their involvement in the Nation of Islam, she never stopped supporting their spiritual journey.

"My mother is a Baptist and when I was growing up she taught me all she knew about God," Ali told his biographer Thomas Hauser. This affection was returned in kind. The stories Odessa would tell about her son demonstrate both a love for her boy and an awe of what he became.

"We called Muhammad 'GG,' when he was born," recalled Odessa, "because you know how babies jabber at the side of their crib—he used to say 'gee gee gee gee'. And then when he became a Golden Gloves champion, he told us, 'You see what that meant? I was trying to say Golden Gloves.' So we called him GG … When he was a child, he never sat still. He walked and talked and did everything before his time … His mind was like the March wind blowing every which way. And whenever I thought I could predict what he would do, he turned around and proved me wrong … He used to stuff cake in his mouth and whenever I thought his mouth was full he'd find a way to say 'More cake mommy more cake.' If I had to spank [his little brother] Rudolph, GG would run in, grab me and say 'Don't hit my baby!' He had confidence in himself and that gave me confidence in him. He started boxing when he was twelve and he would stay up at night telling me how he was going to be the champion some day. It made me nervous watching him in the ring, but I believed he could take care of himself … I always felt like God made Muhammad special, but I don't know why God chose me to carry this child."

Their bond was very strong, and it's easy to see why her influence became so internalized. Cassius could adopt his father's gift of the gab and confidence as an exterior shield to keep reporters, the public, and his entourage at bay, but the people who knew him best always say that when the cameras have gone, and the room is empty, he is himself again, someone who is sweet, shy, and vulnerable. That is Odessa's boy.

Yet his mother's kindness also spurred a different kind of anger in the young Ali; not his father's self destructive fury, aimed at the ones he loved, but anger at a society that would treat such a sweet and harmless woman with abject contempt. The young Ali could not understand why Odessa had to clean white people's homes all day, and then couldn't sit in the front of their buses at night. He couldn't comprehend why his mother wasn't clean enough to use a public restroom, or take a drink at the water fountain.

Ali defined himself by channeling this anger outward instead of against his family or himself, unlike his father. This may be the greatest legacy of Odessa Grady Clay and why she was chosen to carry this child: to raise a man who would never confuse sweetness with weakness, and who would speak out for those denied a seat at the table, not for those who own the restaurant.

She taught us to love people and treat everyone with kindness ... She's a sweet, fat, wonderful woman who loves to cook, eat, make clothes, and be with family. She doesn't drink, smoke, meddle in other people's business or bother anybody and there's no one who's been better to me my whole life.

Right: **Louisville, Kentucky, March 16, 1964**
Ali with his mother Odessa at their Louisville home.

A loyal brother

Leave it to Mr. Cassius Marcellus Clay, Sr., a man of tremendous ego, flair, and showmanship, to name his first son after himself, and his second after the world's greatest lover!

Rudolph Valentino Clay was born in 1944 and from the beginning his two-year-old brother held him tightly. Their mother Odessa remembers disciplining Rudy and seeing Cassius run into the other room screaming, "Please take your hands off my baby!" As Rudy Clay—today known Rahaman Ali—remembered:

Muhammad and I had a few fights between us. All brothers do. But it was nothing serious; more like tests of strength, wrestling. He always had to be the leader, and we let him because he was very intelligent and quick. Outside of boxing, he never played much sports.

In many of the archetypical moments of Muhammad Ali's life, Rahaman was there. When Cassius had his bike stolen, which led him to Officer Joe Martin's Louisville amateur boxing program, Rahaman signed up right alongside him. Like Cassius, Rahaman was one the finest fighters Louisville has ever produced: he just had to live with the fact that he wasn't the Greatest.

Rahaman was good enough to try out for the 1960 Olympic team as a heavyweight. Cassius even worked out to move down to the light-heavyweight division so Rahaman could take his shot amongst the heavies. When Cassius went to his first Nation of Islam meeting, Rudy was right there with him. It was Rudy in fact who joined in advance of his big brother and played a pivotal role in convincing him to be public about his conversion. When Cassius Clay "shook up the world" in defeating the frightening heavyweight champion Sonny Liston on February 25, 1964, Rudy Clay was on the under card in his fight debut, much to Cassius's joy. This scene was immortalized in the *New York Times* by Robert Lipsyte in 1964 who wrote:

"Earlier, rumors had swept Convention Hall that Cassius was not going to show, that the thin line of hysteria he had trod during the morning weigh-in has become full-scale fear. But even as the rumor mounted (that he was in a plane, en route to Mexico), Cassius was standing quietly in a far corner of the arena. He was waiting for his brother, Rudolph Valentino Clay, to make his professional début. Few people noticed him. He was dressed in a tight-fitting black tropical suit and wore a black bow tie on his ruffled, white dress shirt … Bundini kept a hand on Clay's back, as if he might have to restrain him at any moment. But Clay hardly moved. Despite his height (6 feet 3 inches) he often had to stand on tip-toe to watch the action in the far-off ring. Once, when Rudy floored his opponent, Chip Johnson of Naples, Fla., in the second round, Clay shouted some encouragement. Otherwise he was silent."

Rahaman Ali would remain undefeated as he fought sparingly over the next six years. He retired in 1972 after back-to-back losses to Roy Dean Wallace and Jack O'Halloran. Rahaman's record was 12-2-1 with 6 knockouts. He left the fight game with his mind sharp and has been an invaluable commentator on his brother's childhood, on the Louisville of the 1950s, and on their rollicking ride. Rahaman does have one thing Muhammad didn't achieve: a boxing son named Ibn Ali, who is a cruiserweight boxing champion.

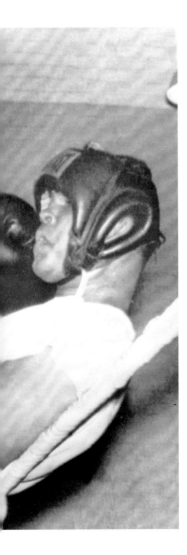

... he was fast. It was hard for the rest of us to make a tag on him because of his speed. ... all the time, he used to ask me to throw rocks at him. I thought he was crazy, but he'd stand back and dodge every one of them. No matter how many I threw, I could never hit him.

Rudy Clay, brother

Left: **Boston, October 29, 1964**
Rudolph Valentino Clay backs his brother Muhammad Ali against the ropes during a training session.

chapter 2
The making of a champion

"I am the greatest!" 1960–1963

By the time Cassius Clay graduated from Louisville Central High School in 1960, he was already an accomplished boxer, with his sights set on both Olympic and championship glory. The previous year he had won a title in the Golden Gloves Tournament of Champions in Chicago, and became the national Amateur Athletic Union light-heavyweight champion. His amateur record was a sparkling 100-5.

Hardly out of school, the 18-year-old Clay was on his way to the Olympic Games in Rome, where on September 5th he defeated the Pole Zbigniew Pietrzykowski to win the light-heavyweight gold medal. Clay's bubbling personality and ever-present camera also won him the adoration of his peers who anointed him "Mayor of Olympic Village." By this time, Clay had signed a professional contract with an all-white consortium of 11 Louisville businessmen led by distillery executive William Faversham. They called themselves the Louisville Sponsoring Group and paid him a $10,000 signing bonus. He used it to buy a pink Cadillac for his parents.

Previous page: **Olympic Games, Rome, September 6, 1960**
A trio of U.S. boxers wear gold medals at the 1960 Olympics. From the left are: Wilbert McClure of Toledo, Ohio; Cassius Clay of Louisville, Kentucky; and Edward Crook of Fort Campbell, Kentucky.
Right: **Olympic Games, Rome, September 14, 1960**
Light heavyweight division winners: Gold medal, Cassius Clay, U.S.A.; silver medal, Z. Pietrzykowski of Poland (far right); bronze medallists, Giulio Saraudi of Italy (left) and Tony Madigan of Australia (second left).

A mind of his own

Clay's sponsors, who collectively knew quite little about boxing, sent him to San Diego to train under the legendary fighter Archie Moore. But Cassius said he wanted to fight like Sugar Ray Robinson, not Moore, and the two proud fighters were unable to forge a working relationship. Moore complained:

My wife is crazy about him, my kids are crazy about him, and I'm crazy about him, but he won't do what I tell him to …

On October 29, 1960, Clay made his pro début, scoring a six-round decision over West Virginia police officer Tunney Hunsaker who immediately became the answer to an eternally asked sports trivia question. By year's end, 37-year-old Angelo Dundee became Clay's trainer, in an association that would stand the test of time.

Clay arrived in Miami in December to work with Dundee who, unlike Moore, did not try to change the young fighter's unorthodox, upright, hands-low style. He did later say that Clay "Ruined a generation of fighters" with this style. In his sixth pro fight, against Lamar Clark on April 19th, Clay predicted—for the first time—the round in which he would defeat an opponent. He fulfilled his promise that "This Clark will fall in two." This would become a staple of his style.

At this point in his life, young Cassius was already looking for spiritual and political answers to the questions he had confronted growing up in the apartheid world of the Jim Crow South. Although raised a Baptist like many southern blacks, in High School he began to explore the ideas of a uniquely American religion called the Nation of Islam, which believed in political, economic, and physical separation from whites. In 1961, at age twenty, he visited a NOI mosque in Miami and later said that this was "the first time in my life that I felt truly spiritual." In 1962, Clay heard Nation of Islam's leader Elijah Muhammad speak for the first time, and also met another Nation of Islam official, Malcolm X, with whom he would have a brief but spectacularly intense friendship.

In a little reported moment, on March 9 of the same year, the military draft board classified Clay 1-A, meaning that he was fit and available to be called into the U.S. Army. But Clay, after scoring 78 on a Select Services IQ test, was subsequently classified as unfit to serve in the U.S. military. He was deeply embarrassed but said, "I said I was the greatest not the smartest." On November 15, Clay met his former trainer, 47-year-old Archie Moore, in Los Angeles, and knocked him out in the fourth round.

In 1963 he appeared on the cover of *Sports Illustrated* for the first time, in the June 10th issue, before his fight against the Brtish boxer Henry Cooper in London. He was to eventually appear on the magazine's cover 35 times, second only to Michael Jordan. From 1960 to 1963 the young fighter amassed an impressive record of 19-0, with 15 knockouts, but his greatest challenges—both inside and out of the ring, were yet to come.

Rome Olympics 1960

The young amateur boxer Clay went from "a little colored boy from Louisville" to the international stage without skipping a beat. If the young Louisville Clay was a "nerd" and substandard student who only fit in at the boxing ring, then "Clay International" was truly a fish that finally found his water. First stop was the 1960 Rome Olympics. Of course, it almost never happened.

"He was afraid of flying," remembered his first trainer, Joe Martin. "When it came time to go to Rome, he said he wasn't gonna fly, and that he wouldn't go. I said, 'Well, you'll lose the opportunity of being a great fighter,' and he said, 'Well, I'm not gonna go.' He wanted to take a boat or something … I calmed him down and convinced him if he wanted to be heavyweight champion of the world that he had to go to Rome and win the Olympics." Martin's son, Joe Junior, told the *Louisville Courier-Journal*, "He finally agreed to fly. But then he went to an army surplus store and bought a parachute and actually wore it on the plane. It was a pretty rough flight, and he was down in the aisle praying with his parachute on."

Clay was on the plane, but that didn't stop him from roaming up and down the aisles like a millenarian preacher signaling the end of the world, praying for safe landing. Amazing that a man who in a few short years would be called by one writer "the first world heavyweight champion," because of his travels to fight in every continent, would be almost stymied by a plane.

Once in Rome, the posture of supreme confidence returned. "You would have thought he was running for Mayor," one teammate opined. "He went around introducing himself and learning other people's names and swapping team lapel pins. If they'd had an election, he would have won in a walk." But none of this would have mattered if Clay couldn't back up the patter and personality with the ability to scramble the brains of his opponents. The young magazine *Sports Illustrated,* the magazine that would build itself on Ali's rise, declared him "the best American prospect for a gold medal [in boxing]," adding, "Clay likes to display supreme confidence by doing intricate dance steps between passages of boxing."

Wilbert "Skeeter" McClure, an early training partner said, "In Rome, he was outgoing but he was seriously into boxing. I don't know of anybody on any team who took it more seriously than he did …He worked for that gold medal. He trained very, very hard. We all did … And certainly, when I watched him train, he was one of the hardest trainers I'd ever seen. In the ring he could dance, but at the Olympic Village, we went to one of the Olympic canteens, and he didn't dance at all. And I went to several parties with him later on, and he didn't dance there either. He just didn't dance. This was part of his shyness around women. I guess he never learned how to dance and was too shy to go out and do it on his own. And looking back—and I believe this; I've told Ali several times—I've told him that he was fated. It's like there was a star when he was born that fated him to do what he was going to do and to have impact on mankind around the globe, and there's nothing he could have done to prevent it and nothing he could have done to make it happen. It's just one of those things … And when you think about this young man's life—when I first saw him when he came to our home in Toledo, his pants were up at his ankles, his sports coat was too short, but it's like the clothing was irrelevant because he glowed. Even then, you knew he was special; a nice, bright, warm, wonderful person."

To make America the greatest is my goal,
So I beat the Russian and I beat the Pole,
And for the U.S.A. won the medal of Gold.
The Greeks said you're better than the Cassius of Old.

Left: **Rome, September 5, 1960**
Cassius Clay (right) in action during the Olympic bout against Z. Pietrzykowski of Poland. Clay outpointed the Pole and won the gold medal.
Next page: **Louisville, Kentucky, September 10, 1960**
Cheering students of Central High School surround Clay, who is proudly wearing his Olympic gold medal.

45

Tarnished gold

After beating the Eastern Bloc strongman, Clay was asked by a Soviet reporter how it felt to win a gold medal for his country when there were restaurants in the United States he could not eat in. His answer tells a great deal because it speaks to his frame of mind at the start of the decade, when Vietnam was France's problem and the black struggle in the U.S. was confined to the south. "Tell your readers we got qualified people working on that problem, and I'm not worried about the outcome. To me, the USA is the best country in the world, including yours," he said.

But behind the boastfulness and bombastic poems, and interviews that were "less like discussions and more like monologues," there was a great deal of pain. Clay returned to Louisville, but found that the color of his medal was not more important than the color of his skin. Clay loved his medal. He would go to sleep wearing it and said he had to learn to sleep on his back, because it could cut his chest when he would roll over.

But when he entered into a Louisville luncheonette and sat down, the owner burst out the back and said, "You get the hell out of here." According to witnesses, a waitress upbraided her manager, saying, "You can't kick him out of here. He's an Olympic champ." The manager ignored her and kicked Clay to the curb. The "The Louisville Lip" left without a sound.

Here is where the story gets murky. In the future Muhammad Ali's autobiography *The Greatest*, as well as in countless interviews, he speaks of throwing his medal in the Ohio River after this affront. Certainly it is easy to imagine someone with the flair for the dramatic and the disregard of the material taking such an action. It also fits in with the dramatic arc of Ali's life: his eternal rejection of the conventional, the mainstream, and the easy path. But this story is probably no truer than George Washington's cherry tree or Abe Lincoln's bear wrasslin'. Most likely, according to both Ali and his closest confidants, the medal was simply lost. Although less dramatic, certainly, it is still quite telling that something that could mean so much to him would be seen as more of a millstone than gold.

But despite this private pain, which later would flower into a historic public political resistance, the young Clay never stopped his funny, endless act. The press didn't quite know what to make of him. They were veterans of the idea that boxers (particularly black boxers) should be doing their talking in the ring. The older writers, called him, with something less than kindness, "The Louisville Lip," "Cash the Brash," "Mighty Mouth," "Claptrap Clay," and "Gaseous Cassius." They also hated his style of dancing around the ring, his hands slung low. A.J. Liebling, the dean of boxing scribes back in the days when they fancied themselves as wordsmiths, wrote:

Clay had a skittering style, like a pebble scaled over water. He was good to watch, but he seemed to make only glancing contact. It is true that the Pole finished the three-round bout helpless and out on his feet, but I thought he had just run out of puff chasing Clay, who had then cut him to pieces... A boxer who uses his legs as much as Clay used his in Rome risks deceleration in a longer bout.

Mugging for the camera

A brand new generation of writers was electrified by the young champ. As legendary U.S. sportswriter Dick Schaap said:

Even at eighteen, Clay was the most vivid, the most alive figure I'd ever met ... It was like meeting a great actor or an electrifying statesman, some sort of figure that had a glow, an energy inside him, and you knew right away that you'd be hearing about him for years.

Clay was absolutely irrepressible. Archie Moore's trainer Dick Sadler said, "First the kid would be standing shouting out of the carriage. 'I am the greatest. I am the greatest!' He'd shout this at passing cars and sheep and fields and stuff. Then after a while he started singing this number by Chubby Checker about the twist. He didn't know the words, just kept on and on singing 'Come on baby, let's do the twist; come on baby, let's do the twist!' And it got to me. It was driving me crazy, to tell you the truth. And I said, 'Jesus, son, you done twisted all across California and Arizona.' By the time we got to New Mexico, I told him, 'Look, sing the Charleston or the Boogaloo or any damned thing, but get off the twist.' Seven hundred miles of twisting, twisting, and 'I am the greatest!' It drove me crazy!"

He was the first athlete to mug for the camera. Television was still a new medium, but young Clay was a pioneer in seeing how the lens could transport him above the pens and scabrous eyes of the boxing literati. As writer Jerry Izenberg commented: Once Ali found out about television, it was, "Where? Bring the cameras! I'm ready now." And as his long time trainer Angelo Dundee said, "You know, it's funny, Muhammad was never as talkative as people thought. In private, even twenty-five years ago, a lot of the time he was real thoughtful and quiet. But he knew how to promote himself. God, he could do that."

In fact Clay never stopped talking. In a less guarded moment, he explained why.

Where do you think I'd be next week if I didn't know how to shout and holler and make the public take notice? I'd be poor and I'd probably be down in my hometown, washing windows or running an elevator and saying 'yassuh' and 'nawsuh' and knowing my place.

Knowing his place was the one thing he never wanted to do. He was helped by having handlers who were very hands off. His future "fight doctor" Ferdie Pacheco always said that Clay had the greatest luck of anyone he ever knew. This was evident early on, as he came along right when the mafia and organized crime, which for so long had a stranglehold on the heavyweight division, was in disarray. Instead he was backed by eleven white men, called the Louisville Sponsoring Group, between the ages of twenty-five and seventy, ten of whom were millionaires or heirs to old-line Kentucky fortunes. Clay received a $10,000 signing bonus and, for the first two years, a guaranteed draw of $333 a month against earnings.

The "training under water" spoof

Neil Leifer recalled Clay's meeting with the *Life* magazine photographer Flip Schulke in 1961. "His eyes widened, and he told Schulke, 'I never told nobody this, but me and Angelo have a secret. Do you know why I'm the fastest heavyweight in the world? I'm the only heavyweight that trains underwater.'

"Schulke said, 'What do you mean?' And Ali explained, 'You know why fighters wear heavy shoes when they run? They wear those shoes because, when you take them off and put the other shoes on, you feel real light and you run real fast. Well, I get in the water up to my neck and I punch the water, and then when I get out of the water, I'm lightning fast because there's no resistance.'

"Schulke was skeptical, but Ali swore it was the truth, and to prove his point, he told Schulke, 'Tomorrow morning, you can see me do it. I do it every morning with Angelo, and no one's ever seen it before. I'll let you photograph it for *Life* magazine as an exclusive.'

"So Schulke called up *Life* and suggested the piece, and I think they ran five pages of Ali up to his neck in a swimming pool. And the two things I remember most about that were, first, Ali couldn't swim, not a bit; and second, Ali had never thrown a punch underwater in his life. It was a total bullshit story he made up, but it got him in *Life*, and *Life* didn't do it as a joke. They were convinced he trained underwater. Now that's a genius you don't see in people very often. Genius and a bit of a con man, too."

Right: **Christie's auction house, London, May 13, 2005**
Collector James Danziger holds Flip Schulke's classic image of Muhammad Ali training underwater. It was expected to sell for up to U.S. $2,800.

Finding a trainer for life

Clay was clear about his early goals which later in life would ring as almost cruel: "I don't want to fight to be an old man. That's all right for you, but I'm gonna only fight five or six years, make me two or three million dollars, and quit fighting."

After several abortive attempts at getting started, he finally found the right fit: a trainer who wouldn't try to change his unorthodox style—Angelo Dundee.

Muhammad Ali still to this today has enormous respect for Dundee. As he told Thomas Hauser, "Angelo Dundee was with me from my second professional fight. And no matter what happened after that, he was always my friend. He never interfered with my personal life. There was no bossing, no telling me what to do and not do, in or out of the ring."

"In a sport not known for its decency," adds Dick Schaap, "Angelo Dundee is a decent man."

But not even Dundee knew how good, how different, Clay could be until former champion Ingemar "Ingo" Johansson came looking for a sparring partner to prepare for a rematch against current champ Floyd Patterson. They thought the skinny Olympic champ would be a good punching bag. They were so wrong.

Left: **Louisville, Kentucky, September 10, 1960**
Gold medal winner Cassius Clay (standing in car) returns home from the Olympics to Louisville, and rides in triumph through the city streets.

We were in the hotel watching television, when the phone rang. And it was this kid saying, 'Mr. Dundee, my name is Cassius Marcellus Clay; I'm the Golden Gloves champion of Louisville, Kentucky.' And he gave me a long list of championships he was planning to win, including the Olympics and the heavyweight championship of the world, and then he said he wanted to come up to the room to meet us. I put my hand over the mouthpiece and said to Willie, 'There's a nut on the phone; he wants to meet you!'

Angelo Dundee

Right: **City Parks Gym, New York, February 8, 1962**
Clay poses for photographers with his trainer, Angelo Dundee.

A decent man in an indecent sport

Angelo Dundee was born Angelo Merena in 1921. He entered the fight game through his brother Chris Dundee, a prominent promoter who opened the legendary 5th Street Gym in Miami, where Angelo became head trainer.

In a fight game marked by hustlers and people striving to squeeze every last dollar from their fighters, Dundee is one of the very few to leave boxing with his reputation intact. While many trainers are infamous for exploiting their charges, Dundee loaned hundreds of thousands of dollars to his fighters throughout their careers. He also was a trainer marked by an absence of ego, which is what made him a perfect Yang for Ali's unbridled Ying.

Dundee knew immediately that the old boxing rules did not apply to Ali, and rather than fit him into a mold, he just had to let him go. As Dundee said to Thomas Hauser, "Training him was a whole different ballgame than with most fighters. You didn't have to push. It was like jet propulsion. Just touch him and he took off. The important thing was, always make him feel like he was the guy. He used to say, 'Angelo doesn't train me.' I didn't. He was right. I directed him and made sure he felt like he was the innovator."

There were always people around Ali, particularly in the Nation of Islam, who encouraged him to dump Dundee. In fact this was one of the few instances where Ali stood up to Elijah Muhammad and insisted that on the subject of who should train him, he knew more than the Messenger. Elijah Muhammad wisely backed away. Ali was self-aware enough to know that Dundee's approach to handling him was tailor made for his style in and out of the ring. He said, years after his retirement, that Angelo Dundee "was there when I needed him and he always treated me with respect. There just wasn't any problem ever between us."

But just because Dundee handled Ali lightly, doesn't mean he was a wilting flower. At several moments when Ali was about to look mortal, it was Dundee who propped him up. In fact, the history of boxing would be quite different if Dundee hadn't insisted young Cassius Clay not quit when Liston blinded him in their first fight, and hadn't kept Muhammad Ali above ground against Joe Frazier in Manila. The credit goes to Ali, as it should, but a lesser trainer would have let him toss in the towel. It could be argued perhaps that a more humane trainer would not have let Ali take such horrific punishment, and this has been said of Dundee. But that is like criticizing a tiger for eating meat. If Dundee wasn't willing to push Ali to victory, both the fighter and his backers would have quickly found a trainer who would.

As intertwined as Dundee's name and career is with Ali, his résumé is profoundly more ornate. Dundee was the force behind welterweight champion Sugar Ray Leonard. The list of noteworthy fighters trained by Dundee also includes George Foreman, Jimmy Ellis, Luis Rodríguez, Sugar Ramos, Ralph Dupas, and Willie Pastrano. Dundee was finally inducted into the International Boxing Hall of Fame in 1992. But that is a rogue's gallery of the first order. A more touching tribute was made by Howard Cosell who once said famously about Dundee: "He is the only man in boxing to whom I would entrust my own son."

Singin' and dancin' training sessions

The Johansson-Clay training sessions were just hilarious. Harold Conrad, sets the scene: "[Clay] says, 'Johansson?' Then he starts singing. 'I'll go dancin' with Johansson. I'll go dancin' with Johansson.' I said to Angelo, 'What the hell is this?' And Angelo says, 'You ain't seen nothing yet with this crazy bastard.'… "Anyway, they got in the ring, and Johansson had a great right hand but two left feet, and Cassius started dancing, popping him. Now remember, Johansson was getting ready to fight for the heavyweight championship, of the world, but Cassius handled him like a sparring partner… And the whole time, Clay doesn't shut up. He keeps talking to Johansson, saying, 'I'm the one who should be fighting Patterson, not you. Come on, here I am; come and get me, sucker. Come on, what's the matter, can't hit me?' Johansson was furious. I mean, he was pissed. He started chasing Clay around the ring, throwing right hands and missing by twenty feet, looking ludicrous."

Finally Ingo's trainer pulled his esteemed fighter out after two rounds. As he stormed out of the building Clay yelled to the heavens, "I went dancin' with Johannson!"

But his "Louisville Lip" persona did not truly mature until a trip to Las Vegas where Clay appeared on the radio with a 47-year-old pro wrestler with badly bleached hair named George Wagner, AKA Gorgeous George.

After seeing Gorgeous George in action, Clay decided he would hoot and holler like never before. Dick Schaap remembered with a smile, "He'd end a training session by going on the ropes and reciting old poetry and talking to the crowd. And while it was very entertaining the first ten times, by the twentieth time you'd say, 'Hey, let's go out to lunch.' But in the early days, when he was fresh, every minute with him was exciting. And even when he got old, it was still more fun being bored by Ali than being fascinated by anybody else."

But his antics didn't stop outside the ring. Clay would predict the round an opponent would fall, saying, "If he's even alive, I'll get him in five." Then if his opponent was looking like a lost cause before the fifth, Clay would drag out the fight to make his prediction come true. This violates the absolute cardinal golden rule of boxing which is that you finish a fight when you finish a fight. It was an approach that gave Dundee no small amount of *tsuris* and moved him to proclaim, "There's only one Cassius Clay—thank God."

Muhammad Ali reveled in both Dundee's ageda and the storm it caused, saying:

I'm the onliest fighter who goes from corner to corner and club to club debating with fans. I've received more publicity than any fighter in history. I talk to reporters till their fingers are sore.

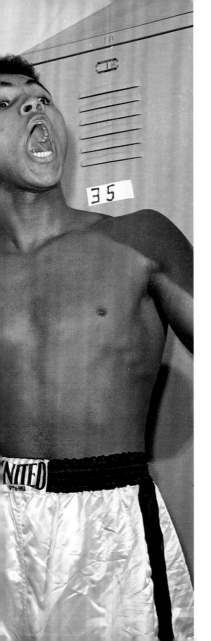

Archie's been living off the
fat of the land,
I'm here to give him his
pension plan.
When you come to the fight,
Don't block the halls and
don't block the door,
Cause ya all going home
after Round Four.

Left: **Los Angeles, November 15, 1962**

Clay points to a sign he has written on a chalk board in his dressing room before his fight against Archie Moore, predicting he would knock Moore out in the fourth round, which is precisely what he went on to do.

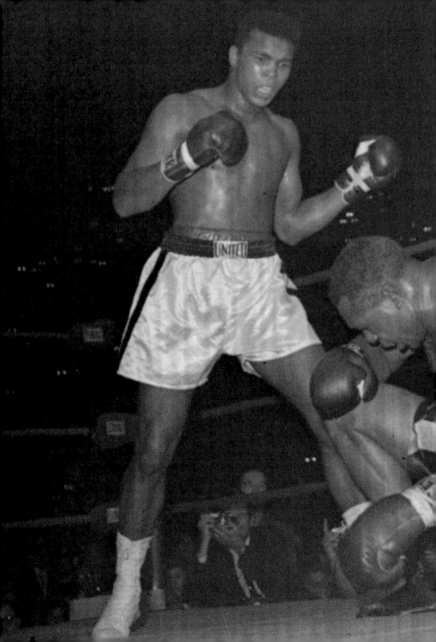

Archie Moore
fell in four.

Left: **Los Angeles, California, November 15, 1962**
Down on one knee, Clay's first professional trainer Archie Moore, now 47 years old, reaches the end of his career as Clay stands over him, winner by a knockout in the fourth round of a scheduled 12-rounder. Moore went down three times before the referee, Tommy Hart, ended the fight.

I'm not the greatest. I'm the double greatest. Not only do I knock 'em out, I pick the round. I'm the boldest, the prettiest, the most superior, most scientific, most skilfullest fighter in the ring today.

Right: **Miami, Florida, February 28, 1963**
Cassius sits with his parents composing a poem predicting that he will knock out Doug Jones in the 6th round of their upcoming New York match.

Inspired by Gorgeous George

There aren't many people in this world that can say they influenced the careers of both Muhammad Ali and Bob Dylan. In fact the point of connection is a man from Seward, Nebraska named George Wagner: known to the world as Gorgeous George. He was a professional wrestler who changed "wrasslin" from a carnival sideshow to "sports entertainment." Gorgeous George realized that by inciting the fans into a frenzy before the opening bell even started, and by projecting an outrageously amplified artifice, he could be far more than his physical skills would allow.

At the age of 24, after wrestling professionally for ten years, George developed a gimmick that catapulted the unimposing 5'9" 215 pounder into the pop culture pantheon. He dyed his hair platinum blonde, grew it down to his shoulders, and kept it perfectly in place with his trademark gold-plated bobby pins. George would be escorted to the ring by one of his "butlers", Thomas Ross or Geoffrey, who would spray the surroundings with disinfectant or perfume, all to the sounds of "Pomp and Circumstance." Then the referee would reach for the Gorgeous One's robe, or other accoutrement, and George would yell, "Get your damn hands off of me!" George would complement this performance with elaborate schemes of rule breaking, which incensed fans to such a degree he could start riots.

Behind the scenes, Gorgeous George was hardly the heel he was in the ring. As wrestling legend Lou Thesz said:"I liked George a lot. He was a real pro. We worked together a couple of times and I never had any problem with him. He'd say, 'Look, you're the champion. Whatever you want is what we're going to do'. He was so professional, so objective. He didn't believe his own publicity. We sold out St. Louis once a week before the match. We had 18,000 people, standing room only, during an ice storm when no one could even walk along the sidewalk. It was unbelievable."

There was no small measure of homophobia in George's act, which stirred the hatred and pressed the psychosexual buttons of fans, but for those who felt in on the joke, or the con—his flamboyance and his ability to press those buttons was genius.

Gorgeous George broke onto the scene at the birth of television and mass culture at the right time, going into homes all over America from Louisville, Kentucky, where Cassius Clay lived, to Hibbing, Minnesota, home of singer Bob Dylan. Young Cassius Clay immediately recognized his genius for self promotion when he appeared on the radio with him in Las Vegas. George was 47 years old and paunchy, but he stole the show.

As Ali remembered, "First, they asked me about my fight. And I can't say I was humble, but I wasn't too loud. Then they asked Gorgeous George about a wrestling match he was having in the same arena, and he started shouting: 'I'll kill him; I'll tear his arm off. If this bum beats me, I'll crawl across the ring and cut off my hair, but it's not gonna happen because I'm the greatest wrestler in the world.' And all the time, I was saying to myself, 'Man, I want to see this fight. It don't matter if he wins or loses; I want to be there to see what happens.'"

Bob Dylan shared Ali's enthuiasm. Early in Dylan's career, Gorgeous George sat in the audience. As Dylan wrote in his autobiography *Chronicles,* "He winked and seemed to mouth the phrase, 'You're making it come alive.' I never forgot it. It was all the recognition and encouragement I would need for years."

... the whole place was sold out when Gorgeous George wrestled. There was thousands of people including me. And that's when I decided I'd never been shy about talking, but if I talked even more, there was no telling how much money people would pay to see me.

Right: **USA, circa 1950**
Autographed publicity postcard featuring Gorgeous George, a.k.a. "The Human Orchid." He was famous for his dyed hair and flamboyant clothing—including wearing sumptuous red velvet robes into the ring.

Gorgeously Yours

Gorgeous George

... I'm king of the world, I'm pretty, I'm pretty!

Left: **Wembley, London, June 18, 1963**

Clay laid his claim to being boxing royalty when he entered the ring for his fight with British heavyweight Henry Cooper. He was resplendent in a crown, and a red and gold robe.

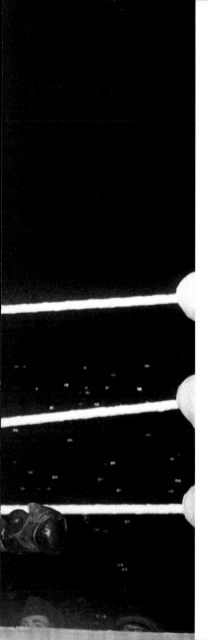

Our 'Enery's capable,
but I think you'll win.

English philospher,
Lord Bertrand Russell

You're not as dumb
as you look!

Cassius Clay's famous riposte

Left: **Wembley Arena, London, June
18, 1963**
Henry Cooper sends Clay
sprawling at the end of the fourth
round with his famous left, known
as "Enery's hammer." Clay was
literally saved by the bell. Angelo
Dundee reported that his glove
had been split. New gloves were
sent for, giving him time to recover,
and he went on to win in the next
round. In England three years
later, Ali again met the 92 year old
philosopher Bertrand Russell, who
wrote to him to express his
support for his stand against the
Vietnam War. They corresponded
until Russell's death in 1970.

chapter 3

Taking a stand

A pivotal year: 1964–1965

In a breathtakingly short time, from 1964 to 1965, Cassius Clay's world turned upside down in the rapid transition from being boxing's new superstar to becoming the most epically reviled star athlete in the history of the United States. Even when he first emerged into the public eye, the press didn't know what to make of the young man they called "The Louisville Lip" and "Gaseous Cassius." But their curiosity turned ugly when rumors swirled, before his February 1964 championship bout against the fearsome Sonny Liston, that he was thinking of joining the Nation of Islam (NOI). Their incessant questioning was so unrelenting that Clay eventually responded "Maybe I will join if you keep asking me!"

In the lead up to the Liston fight Clay was visited by other popular young icons such as the Beatles, the Soul singer Sam Cooke, and the footballer and activist Jim Brown. But the most prominent guest at his training camp was the Nation of Islam speaker Malcolm X who told the press—to jeers—that Clay would defeat Liston. In private, he told Clay that the fight was bigger than boxing: it was "The Cross vs. the Crescent." This would be a recurring theme for Clay: assigning broader political and religious import to his bouts. On February 25 1964, Clay scored a stunning seventh-round defeat over Liston with a technical knockout, winning the world heavyweight championship at age 22. He was the second youngest heavyweight champion in history, trailing only his future

Previous page: **Lewiston, Maine, May 25, 1965**
Ali taunts Sonny Liston, challenging him to get up after knocking him down in the first round of their rematch. The previous year Ali had knocked Liston out in the seventh round to win the heavyweight title.

opponent Floyd Patterson. His pessimistic sponsors, who had planned the quickest route to get Clay to the hospital, failed to arrange a victory celebration. Instead Clay celebrated in Malcolm X's hotel room, hanging out with Jim Brown and Sam Cooke. Over ice cream, they planned to truly "shake up the world."

The day after, Clay responded to a reporter who asked if he was "a card carrying member of the Nation of Islam" by saying that he was. The sports press and the mainstream civil rights community publicly condemned his decision. But Clay was adamant:

I believe in Allah and in peace. ... I'm not a Christian anymore ... I'm free to be whatever I want. ... Followers of Allah are the sweetest people in the world. They don't tote weapons. They pray five times a day.

The next months were a swirl of activity. Casting off his "slave name" Clay traveled to the United Nations and met with African leaders alongside Malcolm X, signing autographs with his self-chosen new name Cassius X. On March 6 he announced that Elijah Muhammad, the leader of the Nation of Islam, had given him the name Muhammad Ali, which means "Praiseworthy One." Granting Clay the name Muhammad Ali was a way for Elijah to woo the young champion to his side in his growing rift with Malcolm X. Ali gradually rejected Malcolm's friendship, a decision he would recall years later with great regret.

Ali was shy with women, and had his first date with Sonji Roy, a cocktail waitress two years his senior. Before the date was over, he proposed. They married on August 14 1964, despite having only known each other for a month.

The following year was equally action packed and controversial. The news that Malcolm X had been assassinated on February 21st in New York hit the headlines. Ali expressed little regret, toeing the official line of the NOI that Malcolm was an apostate.

Professionally, Ali had his new championship to defend. On May 25, 1965, he knocked out Liston in the first round of their rematch, before only 4,280 fans in Lewiston, Maine. Liston fell under a so-called "phantom punch," giving rise to suspicions that the mob-connected boxer threw the fight. After Liston fell, Ali stood over his prostrate body yelling for him to get up, in one of the most famous sports photos in history. The controversy surrounding the bout, and Ali's membership of the NOI, caused former champion Joe Louis to declare Ali "unfit" to hold the title.

On November 22nd of that year, Ali fought Floyd Patterson. In the lead up to the fight, Patterson attacked Ali's religion, politics, and patriotism, saying, among other statements, that "Cassius Clay is disgracing himself and the Negro race." The bout itself turned out to be far less interesting that the verbal sparring, with Ali punishing Patterson over 12 rounds. He was later criticized for—of all things—not knocking Patterson out sooner! Hatred of Ali had become all encompassing in both the mainstream press and main street USA.

To make matters worse, Ali's "idyllic" marriage was falling apart. The headstrong Sonji objected to the influence of the NOI on his finances and personal life—they encouraged him to make her dress "more chastely." They divorced after just 17 months of marriage.

Right: **Lewiston, Maine, May 25, 1965**
Ali and his wife Sonji celebrate his successful title defense against Sonny Liston.

I sparred with Cassius Clay, as he was called then—I taught him everything he knew.

Ringo Starr

Left: **Miami Beach, Florida, February 18, 1964**
Clay, preparing for his championship fight against Sonny Liston, clowns around with the Beatles at his training camp. From the left the Beatles are: Paul McCartney, John Lennon, Ringo Starr, and George Harrison.

The championship: Ali versus Sonny Liston

Sometimes a poster can say more than a thousand words. The ad for the first fight between champion Charles "Sonny" Liston and the young Cassius Clay in January 1964 reveals a boxing cognoscenti completely uninformed about the participants involved. In the poster, Liston is depicted as a fearsome unstoppable brute, his face contorted with a rage so intense it looks like his famed evil eye could kill a puppy at fifty paces.

Clay, on the other hand, is bland, his face a mask of either glassy-eyed fear or even worse, detachment. Unlike Liston who looks poised to either throw a deadly roundhouse or just commence with eating his opponent, Clay looks as if his feet are fastened to the floor like someone standing frozen in front of a moving train. The poster also makes the two look roughly the same height even though, if they had had the occasion to dance, Clay could have rested his chin on Liston's head.

This poster is a valuable artifact because it reflects the reality of how this fight was perceived. Liston was the brute, a former leg-breaker for the mafia who dispatched people with a violence that frightened and entranced observers. Clay was seen as all mouth, someone who would be lucky to make it to the hospital in one piece after the fight.

Right: **Miami Beach, Florida, February 25, 1964**
The Liston-Ali fight poster showing details of how the two fighters measured up for their world heavyweight title bout.

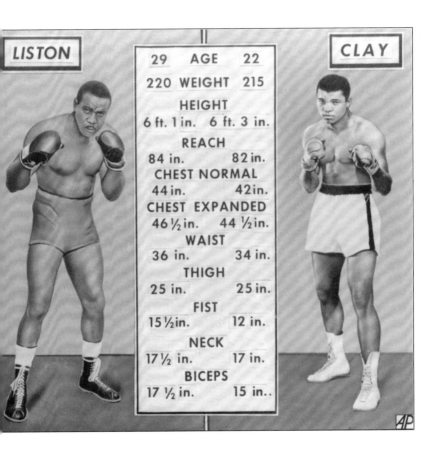

LISTON		CLAY
29	AGE	22
220	WEIGHT	215
	HEIGHT	
6 ft. 1 in.		6 ft. 3 in.
	REACH	
84 in.		82 in.
	CHEST NORMAL	
44 in.		42 in.
	CHEST EXPANDED	
46 ½ in.		44 ½ in.
	WAIST	
36 in.		34 in.
	THIGH	
25 in.		25 in.
	FIST	
15 ½ in.		12 in.
	NECK	
17 ½ in.		17 in.
	BICEPS	
17 ½ in.		15 in..

AP

The sports commentators take sides

In a pre-fight poll of "experts," 93% of all boxing writers believed that the fight would be won by Liston in typical quick and dirty fashion. Les Keiter, reporting on the poll at the time, wrote:

The man who has been screaming to the heavens that he's the greatest meets his destiny—the awesome Liston, a man cut from the mold of Joe Louis; a man who can take a man out with either hand; a ring executioner who has disposed of his opposition in the first round the last three times he has answered the bell. And now, as the electric moment draws near, the more than one hundred writers from all over the globe here for the title clash have gone down the line for the champ, giving the challenger no chance at all.

Bert Sugar, the respected boxing historian, commented years later, "There was only one word for Sonny Liston: invincible."

Harold Conrad said, "When Sonny gave you the evil eye—I don't care who you were—you shrunk to two feet tall. And one thing more. He could fight like hell."

The distinguished sports commentator A.J. Liebling wrote:

Cassius must be kidding. If he isn't, he's crazy to consider entering the ring against a virtually indestructible and demonstrably deadly fighting machine. Clay's style is made to order for a massacre. He carries his hands too low, he leans away from a punch, and he cannot fight a lick inside. He will face in Liston an opponent with endurance, highly developed skills, deceptive speed, and strength enough to stun an elephant with either hand.

An interesting morality play was developing. Boxing had always relied on the black hat/white hat approach to promoting fights. One of the contenders would be set up by promoters and a compliant media to be the bad guy—usually a thug, a brute—and someone else was the good guy who represented mom, apple pie, and the American way. In years past black hat/white hat was as easily identifiable as the boxers' skin color. That changed in 1938 when "The Brown Bomber" Joe Louis struck a blow against fascism by knocking out the German Max Schmeling.

Liston, throughout his whole career, with his background in prison, and among the mob, had always been the man in the black hat. When promoter William McDonald first set up this fight, the young Clay seemed the ideal candidate to wear the white hat, being the golden, handsome, Olympic champion that he was.

But his flamboyant boasts made him repellent to the older generation of sports writers; and this was to be a fight between two boxers whom the media, and the white ticket-buying public, saw as equally distasteful.

Hip-hop opponent-baiting

As for Clay, he didn't back down. On the contrary! In brilliant, self-promoting fashion he released a record on which he recited the following poem—in the style of a mocking, combative hip-hop artist of his day:

Clay comes out to meet Liston
And Liston starts to retreat
If Liston goes back any further
He'll end up in a ringside seat.
Clay swings with a left,
Clay swings with a right,
Look at young Cassius
Carry the fight.
Liston keeps backing
But there's not enough room
It's a matter of time.
There, Clay lowers the boom.
Now Clay swings with a right,
What a beautiful swing,
And the punch raises the bear,
Clear out of the ring.
Liston is still rising
And the ref wears a frown,

For he can't start counting,
Till Sonny comes down.
Now Liston disappears from view.
The crowd is getting frantic,
But our radar stations have picked him up
He's somewhere over the Atlantic.
Who would have thought
When they came to the fight
That they'd witness the launching
Of a human satellite?
Yes, the crowd did not dream
When they laid down their money
That they would see
A total eclipse of the Sonny!

In interviews he said, "I'll hit Liston with so many punches from so many angles he'll think he's surrounded. I don't just want to be champion of the world, I'm gonna be champion of the whole universe. After I whup Sonny Liston, I'm gonna whup those little green men from Jupiter and Mars. And looking at them won't scare me none because they can't be no uglier than Sonny Liston."

Liston is a tramp; I'm the champ. I want that big ugly bear. I want that big bum as soon as I can get him. I'm tired of talking. If I can't whip that bum, I'll leave the country.

Gas, gas, gas!

Clay poked fun at Liston's psychologically sensitive points. It was known that Liston, growing up in extreme poverty, didn't have a birth certificate, his age being in perennial doubt like a Cuban émigré ball player today. Cassius railed, "You're 40 years old if you are a day, and you don't belong in a ring with Cassius Clay."

Jim Murray, the esteemed columnist for the *LA Times* reflected the dominant view when he said, "It will be the most popular fight since Hitler and Stalin, 180 million people rooting for a double knockout."

But for the young sportswriters, Clay was a gas, gas, gas. Prefiguring the generation gap that was about to define the country, the young writers had at last found someone who could fill their notebooks and have a blast.

One of these writers was a baby-faced *New York Times* sports scribe named Robert Lipsyte. Lipsyte wasn't even supposed to cover Clay in Miami but got the gig when the senior writer threw it to the kid thinking it would be a dreadful bore. Lipsyte spoke to the generation gap between younger and older writers when he said,

Clay was unique but it wasn't as if he were some creature from outer space for me. For Jimmy Cannon, he was, pardon the expression, an uppity nigger, and he could never handle that…. What Clay did was make guys stand up and decide which side of the fence they were on

It's important for us to remember, particularly in this day and age of hype and sound bites, that reporters had never really seen anything like this before. In African-American culture Clay was using his own variation of a calling-out ritual known as "playing the dozens." Black Baseball League players were rarely if ever covered by the mainstream press, and they would insult one another with good cheer, and also to get a performer's edge. Satchel Paige, the great baseball pitcher was a master at this. But on the bigger stage of boxing, this was completely new, and the old school reporters were not having it.

Another person not having it was Mr. Liston himself. Liston was not a fan of verbosity or fancy talk. His response was very simple.

"I think I'm gonna have to hurt that boy bad." In a famous story, Liston, who trained in the prison yards, went up to Clay in a Vegas casino and slapped the young challenger across the face in clear public view. As Clay froze, Liston said, "Now I got your heart."

But Clay was cut from different stuff. He simply decided that, since he was terrified of Liston anyway, he might as well make him think he was out of his mind. It was calculated, groundbreaking, and completely insane.

For Liston it started when his plane landed in Miami for training. There was Ali screaming in front of reporters, "Chump! You big ugly bear! I'm gonna whup you right now!" Then he followed Liston's car, aggravating Liston to the point of pulling off the road, getting out of the car and threatening Cassius, in a cold, low voice, with serious bodily harm. Clay just got his phalanx of people to conveniently pull him away while he shouted, "Come on Punk! This ain't no joke! Right now!"

Then Clay started sending people to Liston's training camp with picket signs saying things like, "We all LOVE Cassius Clay!" "March on Liston's Camp" and "Bear Huntin'."

Sonny Liston is nothing. The man can't talk. The man can't fight. The man needs talking lessons. The man needs boxing lessons. And since he's gonna fight me, he needs falling lessons.

Right: **Boston, Massachusetts, November 9, 1964**

Cassius Clay hams it up, clutching a rope and bear collar, pretending to hunt "the bear"—the nickname of his opponent Sonny Liston. Meanwhile, one of his handlers pours honey on the ground, They are waiting for Liston to appear for his pre-fight physical examination.

Crazy or what?

All this psychological baiting served the purpose of unnerving Liston, who had not trained hard for the fight at all. Remembering the look of abject fear on the young fighter's face in Vegas, he thought he would just have to do what he did to his other opponents— "put the evil eye on him" and watch him run.

But if Liston wondered whether Clay was crazy before, the weigh-in convinced him forever. As Thomas Hauser describes, "What happened was, at 11:09 A.M. Clay reentered the weigh-in room. Two minutes later, Liston appeared, and the challenger seemingly went wild. 'I'm ready to rumble now,' he screamed. 'I can beat you anytime, chump! Somebody's gonna die at ringside tonight! You're scared, chump! You ain't no giant! I'm gonna eat you alive!' Bundini was shrieking, 'Float like a butterfly, sting like a bee.' Dundee, Robinson, and William Faversham were holding on to Clay, who seemed ready to attack Liston at any moment."

As Lipsyte described years later, "[I]t was an absolutely extraordinary performance, because Liston took comfort in the fact that everybody was scared of him. I mean, who wouldn't be terrified of Sonny Liston? Well, the answer, of course, was a crazy person wouldn't be afraid, and now Liston thought Clay was crazy."

Liston wasn't alone. Joe Louis's wife was heard to say in a nervous tone, "This boy is a lunatic! He needs a psychiatrist!"

Clay was fined $2,500 on the spot. As wild as his performance was, it was an act of supreme calculation. His blood pressure during the weigh in was 120 beats per minute, his normal pulse was 54 beats per minute. The ring doctor said, "This young man might be scared to death … If this is his pulse at fight time, the whole thing is off." Yet an hour after the weigh in it was back to 54 beats. It was theater, pure and simple, with only Cassius Clay in on the act. Ali later said, "I didn't want nobody thinking nothing except that I was a joke." Mort Sharnik said, "Nobody could read this kid. He was either the craziest kid you ever saw, or the smartest."

Amazingly, the writers who had spent years harpooning the "terrifying thug" Liston now turned to his side. Jimmy Cannon wrote, "The loudmouth from Louisville is likely to have a lot of vainglorious boasts jammed down his throat by a hamlike fist belonging to Sonny Liston." Murray Kempton aptly explained the racial politics behind the shift. "Liston used to be a hoodlum. Now he was our cop. He was the big Negro we use to keep sassy Negroes in line."

But Liston couldn't keep Clay in line any more than cops were able to keep the new generation in line on college campuses and the inner cities. This was especially the case come fight time.

There was a moment right before the fight where Liston came face to face with Clay and it was obvious that he had never quite realized how tall his opponent was. His famed evil eye was doing little more than staring at Clay's lower lip. Liston was used to being the Bully. The poster had made Clay look like a Middleweight. But the truth was that not only speed but power and size would be in Ali's corner.

For the first two rounds Liston tried to catch Clay with a left jab and he missed Clay like a pitcher with a wild fastball. Then as Clay's trainer Dundee said, "Liston just got frustrated. And when you get frustrated, it takes the snap out of your shots." With Liston out of shape, he resorted to an old trick of rubbing a gel on his gloves, blinding Clay for two rounds. Almost like a Jedi knight Clay was effectively blindfolded trying to keep the power puncher at bay. "It was scary," remembered Dundee "He was blind!"

"Eat your words!"

Dundee realized the trouble his fighter was in, washed the gel out, and got him back up, shielding the ref from the crisis in the corner. At that point, in the words of Burt Sugar, "Liston tried every trick in the book, nothing worked so he said, 'Oh the hell with it.'" Liston, "The Big Ugly Bear" quit on his stool after the seventh, avoiding the ignominy of going down in Clay's predicted eighth round.

Clay went nuts, leaping all around the ring, yelling to anyone who would listen:

"I shook up the world!" "I'm pretty! I'm pretty! I'm a baaadddd man!" "I am the king! The King of the world! Eat your words!

The fight was over. Amazingly this historic fight that "shook up the world" almost never took place. Ironically it was threatened by promoters' concerns at the very religious and political transformation from which Clay drew his strength to hunt Liston down. For behind the fighter with the big mouth, a radical drama was unfolding that, more than any fight in a ring, would truly shake up the world.

Previous page: **Convention Hall, Miami Beach, Florida, February 25, 1964**
Clay smashes a straight left into the face of Sonny Liston in the third round of their heavyweight championship fight. The 22-year-old Clay defeated Liston in a technical knockout to become the second youngest world heavyweight champion ever.
Right: **Convention Hall, Miami Beach, Florida, February. 25, 1964**
Clay's handlers hold him back as he reacts after he is announced the new heavyweight champion of the world.

Celebrating victory with the King of Soul

Few people in the history of recorded music can match the resonance and influence of the amazing Sam Cooke. Born Samuel Cook in Clarksdale, Mississippi, (he added the "e" later,) the future King of Soul started his musical career as a gospel prodigy in his father's church. Cooke went on to fuse gospel and rhythm & blues into what would be known simply as Soul. He recorded classic songs like "You Send Me", "Chain Gang," "Wonderful World" and "Bring It On Home To Me." Cooke was the focus of tremendous pride in the Black community.

He was experimenting with his singular voice, but he was also keeping interesting political company: particularly that of Cassius Clay and Malcolm X. Cooke and Clay were musing about collaborating on an album. In February 1964, Cooke made the trip to Miami to see Clay fight for the title against Sonny Liston. Cooke loved Clay for his sense of daring and unwillingness to play by the old rules. Clay loved Cooke because he turned into a giddy fan around soul singers like Cooke and Lloyd Price.

Immediately after Clay shook up the world by dispatching Liston, he spotted Cooke in the audience. While TV and radio reporters were trying to hold his attention, Clay was focused on having his hero Mr. Cooke come up to share his spotlight. As Peter Guralnick wrote in his book *Dream Boogie: The Triumph of Sam Cooke:* "Cassius was in the middle of an interview … when he spotted Sam, almost disheveled with excitement, his tie removed, shirt open. 'Sam Cooke!' the new champion called out with unabashed enthusiasm. 'Hey, let that man up here.' …'This is Sam Cooke!' Cassius shouted … 'Let Sam in,' he insisted with all the fervor he had put into the fight. 'This is the world's greatest rock 'n'roll singer.' 'We gonna shake up the world!'" the champ called out one more time. "You're beautiful," said Sam, his face wreathed in smiles, his expression one of innocent mirth."

After the fight, Clay had nowhere to go because his promoters, not expecting a victory, didn't plan for a victory celebration. Instead he went back to Malcolm X's hotel to eat vanilla ice cream with Malcolm, Cooke, and football great and political activist Jim Brown.

An undercover FBI informant somberly noted Cooke's presence as a sign that Black radicalism could possibly find voice in the sports and entertainment industries. The next evening, Cooke and Clay finally recorded their album.

As Guralnick commented, "The song Sam had put together to showcase the champion's limited singing skills was called "Hey Hey, The Gang's All Here" and was little more than a variation on the age-old party chant. The one departure was a litany of place-names that evoked the classic R&B instrumental "Night Train," with the singer calling out "Is Memphis with me? Is Louisville with me? Is Houston with me?" and the large backup chorus responding loudly and enthusiastically each time. They worked hard at it, with Sam supplying the energy and direction and keeping everybody's spirits up while Cassius recited poetry and played the drums in between takes. And in the end, everyone walked out of the studio convinced that they had participated in something memorable if not musically significant."

Later that year Cooke was murdered. Like Malcolm X and Martin Luther King, he was killed just as he was beginning to explore a more radical set of beliefs. The song "A Change is Gonna Come" was Cooke's last gift to the world, and it's painful to listen to it without imagining what other wonderful music he would have given to us.

It's been too hard living, but I'm afraid to die
I don't know what's up there beyond the sky
It's been a long time coming
But I know a change is gonna come

Sam Cooke, "A Change is Gonna Come"

Left: **Soul singer-songwriter Sam Cooke, location unknown, circa 1964**
Cooke was the first artist to take a political stand by refusing to sing to segregated audiences. He was a Black nationalist and a great friend of both Muhammad Ali and Malcolm X. He had secretly converted to Islam and became one of the first Black artists to start his own record label.

The Nation of Islam

The Nation of Islam has been a highly controversial religious/political group since its founding in 1930. It is a uniquely home grown American faith system, a reaction to the specific experience of racism in the United States. Its origins begin with Wallace Fard Muhammad, who started what was originally called the Temple of Islam in Detroit at the start of the Great Depression. His temple had many derivations from the Muslim religion as it is practiced throughout the world. It was a mix of Islam and teaching from the Koran with a strain of Black Nationalism that stressed separatism and racial supremacy. Fard Muhammad taught that African-Americans were the earth's "original men" but had been duped out of their global kingdom by genetically bred "white devils." These teachings appealed to many blacks who felt dehumanized by an atmosphere where racist violence was a fact of life.

Fard Muhammad was arrested and deported in 1934, but not before he met his most important acolyte, an unemployed auto worker named Elijah Poole. Poole was born in Georgia, a child of sharecroppers who were once slaves. He had 12 brothers and sisters. The young Elijah Poole spoke of seeing three lynchings before the age of twenty, not an outlandish claim in the Georgia of his day. Poole changed his name to Elijah Muhammad and became the Supreme Minister of the renamed Nation of Islam. In 1942 he went to prison for four years for refusing induction into the army for World War II. This central belief that the Black man had no place in a white man's army would find an echo in the life of Cassius Clay.

Once out of prison, Muhammad became known as someone who took white supremacy and turned it on its head. As one writer wrote, "If whites said blacks were inferior, he would assert instead that whites were the inferior ones. If whites said blacks were cursed, he would state instead that whites were cursed. If whites said 'black' was associated with bad, he would say instead 'white' was associated with bad."

The NOI stood for the complete separation from white America in religion, economics, and politics. They called for a separate black state. In this regard, it was part of a strong tradition of Black Nationalism in the U.S. as seen in the mass movement of Marcus Garvey's United Negro Improvement Association of the 1920s. The difference was the virulence with which the NOI attacked not only white America, but also integrationist Black leaders, and Blacks themselves who lived "unclean" lives, through their diet, drinking, or philandering. At its peak, the organization had 100,000 members.

In *The Fire Next Time,* James Baldwin wrote: "Elijah Muhammad has been able to do what generations of welfare workers and committees and resolutions and reports and housing projects and playgrounds have failed to do: to heal and redeem drunkards and junkies, to convert people who have come out of prison and to keep them out, to make men chaste and women virtuous, and to invest both the male and the female with pride and a serenity that hang about them like an unfailing light. He has done all these things, which our Christian church has spectacularly failed to do."

The Nation's most spectacular period of growth was in the 1950s. At that time, when the most basic rights—the right not to have to give up one's seat on the bus, the right not to have to drink from a separate water fountain, and the right to vote—were met with relentless violence and terror, the Nation offered an alternative. It was a mystical, highly unrealistic alternative, but an alternative nonetheless at a time when separatism seemed like an act of self-preservation.

Why don't we get out and build our own nation? White people just don't want their slaves to be free. That's the whole thing. Why not let us go and build ourselves a nation? … we'll never be free until we own our own land.

Left: **Nation of Islam Convention, Chicago, March 1, 1965**
Ali stands and applauds Elijah Muhammad after his closing address to the convention.

Risking all for his faith

Just before his championship bout with Sonny Liston, Cassius Clay had stared into a professional abyss. He had worked his whole life for a shot at the world heavyweight title, and days before his fight against Liston, promoter William McDonald wanted to call the whole thing off. McDonald was not shy about expressing his frustrations. This fight was supposed to be the cleancut, handsome Olympic champion Cassius Marcellus Clay against the "terrifying thug" Liston. But as Clay himself would say, "I am not going to be who you want me to be." Less than half the seats had been sold, and it was Clay's fault.

It was an open secret that Clay was in a full-scale flirtation with the Nation of Islam, often referred to in the press as the "Black Muslims." The NOI believed in black separatism and that white people were devils, and it organized armed self-defense against racist attacks. Clay started to show up at NOI rallies in the lead up to the fight. The media wanted to know if he was a member and Clay said:

No I'm not (a Muslim), not now. But the way you keep pressing me I just might be.

Reporters were also in a constant state of agitation over the presence of the NOI's most prominent member, Malcolm X, in Clay's camp.

McDonald was furious and told Clay that he would either have to publicly denounce the NOI or the fight was off. Clay looked at McDonald and said, "My religion is more important to me than this fight" and McDonald actually sent Clay home to pack his bags.

The publicist Harold Conrad challenged McDonald's decision saying, "Bill you don't know what you're doing. You will go down in history as a man who denied a man his fight for the title because of his religion." McDonald backed down but only on the condition Malcolm X would leave town. Malcolm readily agreed, but returned for the fight. Many of the people around Clay were shocked that he would risk everything for a "new flirtation" with a "cult." But Clay's fascination with the NOI had been ongoing since he was a high school teenager. As David Remnick wrote:

Clay stunned his English teacher at Central High when he told her he wanted to write his term paper on the Black Muslims. She refused to let him do it … Something had resonated in his mind, something about the discipline and bearing of the Muslims, their sense of hierarchy, manhood, and self-respect, the way they refused to smoke or drink or carouse, their racial pride."

Clay's extensive training in Miami only solidified his commitment to these ideas. Today, Miami is defined by the South Beach party scene, composed of elderly Jews, and large Cuban and Haitian populations. But back then it was a typical Southern town, even more segregated and brutal than Louisville. Clay found himself harassed by police on his morning jogs, and "the greatest" couldn't eat in the town's average restaurants.

Welcome to the brotherhood!

In Dade County's impoverished Black community, he found a sense of both solidarity and protection. Ferdie Pacheco remembered that "He began training in Miami with Angelo Dundee, and Angelo put him in a den of iniquity called the Mary Elizabeth Hotel, because Angelo is one of the most innocent men in the world and it was a cheap hotel. The place was full of pimps, thieves, and drug dealers. And here's Cassius, who comes from a good home, and all of a sudden he's involved with this circus of street people. At first, the hustlers thought he was just another guy to take to the cleaners; another guy to steal from; another guy to sell dope to; another guy to fix up with a girl. He had this incredible innocence about him, and like everybody does, they started to feel protective of him. If someone tried to sell him a girl, the others would say, 'Leave him alone; he's not into that.' If a guy came around, saying, 'Have a drink,' it was, 'Shut up, he's in training.' But that's the story of Ali's life. He's always been a little kid, climbing out onto tree limbs, sawing them off behind him, and coming out okay."

Clay started attending Nation of Islam meetings, where he developed a sense of identity grander than "boxer" or even "Christian." He remembered one preacher, Brother John, saying,

Why are we called Negros? It's the white man's way of taking away our identities. If you see a Chinaman coming, you know he's from China. If you see a Cuban coming, you know he comes from Cuba. If you see a Canadian coming, you know he comes from Canada. What country is called Negro?

Often biographers of Ali, most of them white, dwell luridly on some of the fantastical religiosity of the NOI and scoff openly at how anyone could be attracted to a religion that speaks of a large headed scientist named Yacoob, breeding white devils, and spaceships designed to whisk away the chosen enlightened Blacks. Stanley Crouch said Ali had joined "a gaggle of lunatics." The famed Dick Schaap focused on how impressionable the young fighter was, saying, "At the time, Cassius Clay was quite malleable. I say only half kiddingly that I could have converted him to Judaism if I tried hard enough."

But this analysis of focusing on the personal misses the larger picture of why the NOI was so enticing to someone like Clay. The Nation called for racial pride at a time of degradation. Clay, like many African-Americans of the day, was witnessing a country where "integrationist" blacks were attacked for aspiring to the most simple rights. In this atmosphere, separatism seemed like an act of self-preservation.

Clay's mother, the devout Odessa was distraught at her son's new faith, but as Ferdie Pacheco said, "His mother's church had blacks sit in the back. That's no kind of church. Muhammad's church said black is best."

The most concrete thing I found in churches was segregation … Well, now I have learned to accept my own and be myself. I know we are original man and that we are the greatest people on planet Earth and our women the queens thereof.

The Malcolm X factor

The teachings of the Nation had another benefit for Clay in the lead up to the championship fight. They gave him the purpose and strength to believe he could defeat Liston, embodied in intense friendship with Malcolm X. Malcolm was then in a feud with the Nation of Islam leader Elijah Muhammad. He had been suspended for saying "The chickens have come home to roost" after the assassination of President John F. Kennedy, but the feud was far more complicated than that one infamous statement. It was rooted in both Malcolm's frustration at the NOI's lack of direct political action and the moral hypocrisy he saw in Elijah Muhammad's personal life. During this difficult time, Malcolm saw a lot of himself reflected in the young Clay. Both were charismatic, cutting edge personalities who lived in a media storm of criticism, but they both expressed tremendous love for an increasingly combative and confident Black community.

Malcolm X's charisma was legendary. As Gerald Early wrote:

While Black Nationalist and separatist ideas coming from Elijah Muhammad seemed cranky, cultlike, backwaterish and marginal, the same ideas coming from Malcolm seemed revolutionary, hip, and vibrant.

Right: **Trans-Lux Newsreel Theater, New York, March 1, 1964**
Ali signing autographs soon after defeating Sonny Liston to become World Heavyweight Boxing Champion at the age of 22. He is accompanied by Nation of Islam leader Malcolm X. They had just watched a screening of Ali's fight with Liston.

Malcolm and Cassius became fast friends. When Malcolm joined Clay in Miami, he did so over the objections of Elijah Muhammad who saw Clay as someone who would probably lose to Liston and bring embarrassment onto the NOI. Ferdie Pacheco said, "Malcolm X and Ali were like very close brothers. It was almost like they were in love with each other. Malcolm thought Ali was the greatest guy he ever met and Ali thought he was the smartest black man on the face of the earth because everything he said made sense. Malcolm X was bright as hell, convincing, charismatic, in the way great leaders and martyrs are … The Muslims filled a deep need in Ali. Especially Malcolm."

Malcolm imbued Clay with the idea that he would win because of larger powers at work. He was the first person to set in Clay's mind something that would constantly reappear in his fights: the idea that these boxing matches were higher callings meant to represent larger social battles that made his victory as inevitable as the tide of history. Malcolm said to Clay:

This fight is the truth. It's the cross and the crescent fighting in a prize ring for the first time. It's a modern crusade—a Christian and a Muslim facing each other … do you think Allah has brought all this about intending for you to leave the ring as anything but champion?

In Miami, Malcolm was a lightning rod for reporters, especially after saying, "Clay will win. He is the finest Negro athlete I have ever known and he will mean more to his people than Jackie Robinson. Many people know the quality of mind he has in there. One forgets that although the clown never imitates a wise man, a wise man can imitate the clown."

These statements were not merely for the benefit of the media. Malcolm was attempting to do with Clay what he had done with legions of Blacks: give them a sense that they held a deeper spiritual and cultural superiority that they could call upon for strength.

Betty Shabazz, Malcolm X's wife, remembered:

Cassius was a nervous wreck. He had a great deal of apprehension about fighting Sonny Liston. But my husband talked to him like a little brother and helped him conquer his fear. And this was after Malcolm had been cautioned not to go. He was told by Elijah Muhammad that, if he went, it would be on his own as an individual, not representing the Nation of Islam; and that, if he had good sense, he would stay away, because there was no way Cassius Clay could win. But Malcolm felt that, if Cassius Clay was totally focused on the fight, he could win. And one of the things he said to me was, 'If he loses, he should not be alone.'

Official champion of the Nation of Islam

He didn't lose. After the fight, Clay "shook up the world" once again as he officially announced that he was a member of the Nation of Islam. There are no words to describe the firestorm this caused. Not surprisingly, the men of the conservative, mobbed-up, corrupt fight world lost their minds.

Jimmy Cannon, wrote: "The fight racket since its rotten beginnings has been the red light district of sports. But this is the first time it has been turned into an instrument of hate." Clay was attacked not only by the sports world, but also by the respectable wing of the civil rights movement. Roy Wilkins, of the older civil rights generation said, "Cassius Clay may as well be an honorary member of the white citizen councils."

Clay's response at this point was very defensive. He repeatedly said that his wasn't a political, but a purely religious conversion. His defense reflected the conservative politics of the NOI. Ali said, "I'm not going to get killed trying to force myself on people who don't want me. Integration is wrong. White people don't want it, the Muslims don't want it. So what's wrong with the Muslims? I've never been in jail. I've never been in court. I don't join integration marches and I never hold a sign."

But in tune with Malcolm X, who at the time was engineering a political break from the Nation of Islam, Clay—much to the anger of Elijah Muhammad—found it completely impossible to explain his religious world view without speaking to the mass Black freedom struggle that was happening in the world outside the boxing ring. He was his own worst enemy—claiming that his was a religious transformation and had nothing to do with politics, but then in the next breath saying:

I ain't no Christian. I can't be when I see all the colored people fighting for forced integration get blown up. They get hit by the stones and chewed by dogs and then these crackers blow up a Negro Church … People are always telling me what a good example I would be if I just wasn't Muslim. I've heard over and over why couldn't I just be more like Joe Louis and Sugar Ray. Well they are gone and the Black man's condition is just the same ain't it? We're still catching hell.

Malcolm pointed out the hypocrisy of a white press that excused boxers for all manner of sin, graft, and sloth, but was coming down on the young champ. "Brother Cassius will never do anything that will in any way tarnish or take away from his image as the heavyweight champion of the world. He is trying his best to live a clean life and project a clean image. But despite this, you will find that the press is constantly trying to paint him as something other than what he actually is. He doesn't smoke. He doesn't drink. He's never been involved in any trouble. His record is clean. If he was white, they'd be referring to him as the all-American boy."

But if the establishment press was outraged, a new generation of activists was electrified. As civil rights leader Julian Bond reminisced:

"I remember when Ali joined the Nation. The act of joining was not something many of us particularly liked. But the notion that he would do it, that he'd jump out there, join this group that was so despised by mainstream America and be proud of it, sent a little thrill through you … He was able to tell white folks for us to go to hell; that I'm going to do it my way."

What's in a name?

After he won the title, Clay, started signing autographs as Cassius X or Cassius X Clay. He visited the United Nations with Malcolm X saying "I'm champion of the WHOLE WORLD!" He met diplomats friendly to Malcolm from Liberia, Mali, Gambia and Congo, and announced that he would tour Asia and Africa. His companion would be, he announced grandly, "The Minister Malcolm X."

Elijah Muhammad then took the extraordinary step of "renaming" Cassius Clay as Muhammad Ali. Being renamed was the highest honor that could be bestowed in the Nation, usually granted after years of loyal service. Malcolm immediately saw it as a political move to ensure the Champ would stay with the Nation after Malcolm's imminent expulsion. It was successful, as the newly named Muhammad Ali turned his back on his now ex-friend, saying, "You just can't buck Mr. Muhammad and get away with it."

Ali has taken tremendous criticism in biographies for rejecting Malcolm. But certainly it's worth looking at the broader context of his decision—not to excuse, but to understand.

As Sonia Sánchez has said, "Ali had no time for analysis. He had to make a split-second decision between Malcolm and Elijah Muhammad and there was no gray area, no in-between. He was surrounded by powerful people from the Nation who could convince him that Malcolm may have been close to him, but the real leader was Elijah Muhammad. Also remember that the split was not helped by the way outside forces including the FBI, infiltrated the Nation and other Black groups … Ali was a great man, but he was not a thinker, an analyst, You couldn't expect him to make flash decisions better than anyone else." Also it is worth keeping in mind that Ali would have risked his life by standing with Malcolm. Ali was the first heavyweight champion in years—or perhaps ever—not to be run by the mob. The Muslims were his muscle to prevent the mob from moving in on him. To repel the NOI is a lot to ask a 22 year old.

Some have even taken the rather extraordinary step of blaming Ali for Malcolm's 1965 assassination. This is done by writers who seem to have no love for Malcolm X except in this narrow instance. Once again, given what we know about FBI infiltration, J. Edgar Hoover's paranoid fears of a "black messiah," collusion between the NOI and government assassins, this is a charge rooted more in burying Ali's legacy than examining it.

But despite all of this drama, the internal politics of the Nation were not what was capturing the attention of the boxing public and media. The man had changed his name to something Islamic and foreign. Many leading publications, like the *New York Times*, had a policy for years against using his new name. Initially many poor Blacks didn't know what to make of this either. As George Foreman said in an interview with me,

"When I first heard about it, all I ever heard anyone saying in the fifth ward [in Houston] was, 'How could that boy change his name? What is that boy doing?' Then we heard he was a Black Muslim. My community was afraid of that word. Not the word Muslim, the word Black! The word frightened everybody. No one had heard the word Black in Texas to describe a so-called "Negro" at that time. Everyone was saying he was crazy. Then there were some people who said, 'I would like to meet him, to talk to him, to hear what he had to say.' I just had admiration for him at the time. You would hear about him being on the radio and you would just tear home no matter what was going on."

Clay has every right to follow any religion he chooses and I agree. But, by the same token, I have every right to call the Black Muslims a menace to the United States and a menace to the Negro race. I do not believe God put us here to hate one another. Cassius Clay is disgracing himself and the Negro race.

Floyd Patterson

Left: **Baltimore, Maryland, May 6, 1964**
Ali, recently honored with the new name, Muhammad Ali, by Nation of Islam leader Elijah Muhammad, waves a copy of the Black Muslim newspaper *Muhammad Speaks*.

Muhammad Ali: a powerful political force

Comedian and social commentator Dick Gregory said of Ali:

A lot of people were afraid because he changed his name. You can't change your name. It's an awful thing to do to change your name. You don't believe that? Ask Coca-Cola. Tell them to change their name.

Almost overnight, whether you called him Ali or Clay, he became a political question in barber shops, bars, and on street corners. How a person referred to the champ in casual conversation said what side they were on in the struggles taking place in the broader society.

During the summer of 1964, there were 1,000 arrests of civil rights activists, 30 buildings bombed and 36 churches burned by the Ku Klux Klan and their sympathizers. In 1964, too, the first of the urban uprisings and riots in the northern ghettoes took place.

The politics of Black Power was starting to emerge and Ali was a critical symbol in this transformation. As news anchor Bryant Gumbel said, "One of the reasons the civil rights movement went forward was that Black people were able to overcome their fear. And I honestly believe that for many Black Americans, that came from watching Muhammad Ali. He simply refused to be afraid. And being that way, he gave other people courage."

A concrete sign of Ali's early influence was seen in 1965 when Student Non-Violent Coordinating Committee (SNCC) volunteers in Lowndes County, Alabama launched an independent political party. Their new group was the first to use the symbol of a black panther.

Their bumper stickers and T-shirts were of a black silhouette of a panther and their slogan was straight from the champ: "We Are the Greatest."

Famed civil rights activist Lawrence Guyot said to me once with a trembling passion:

You have to put yourself in our shoes. We were down there in these small, hot dusty Southern towns, in an atmosphere thick with fear, trying to organize folk whose grandparents were slaves. A town where you had the Klan on one side, the local sheriff's department on the other and more than a little intermingling between the two. And here was this beautifully arrogant young man who made us proud to be us and proud to fight for our rights.

This movement became a global phenomenon when Ali visited Africa, albeit without Malcolm X, as a champion. In Ghana he met President Kwame Nkrumah and throngs of Ghanaians shouting the name that the U.S. press was refusing to use: "Ali." Poet Maya Angelou, living in Ghana at the time said, "All of a sudden he belonged to them as well."

In his travels through Africa, he also came across Malcolm X. Ali rudely rebuffed Malcolm, wounding him deeply. But Malcolm still sent him a note that was prophetic, and perhaps influential to some of Ali's later choices. It simply read, "Because billions of our people in Africa, Asia, and Arabia, love you blindly. You must be forever aware of your responsibility to them."

It was during this trip that Ali came to understand that he was accountable to a broader, international constituency, a constituency of the oppressed, and this new sense of accountability was to guide him over the next turbulent decade.

Mike Marqusee

Left: **Kennedy Airport, New York, May 15, 1964**
Heavyweight boxing champion Muhammad Ali waves as he leaves for Accra, Ghana. He is beginning an eight-week tour of African and Asian countries accompanied by Rahaman (Rudy) Ali, his brother.

The great legacy of Malcolm X

"Malcolm was our manhood, our living, black manhood! This was his meaning to his people. Consigning these mortal remains to earth, the common mother of all, secure in the knowledge that what we place in the ground is no more now a man but a seed, which, after the winter of our discontent, will come forth again to meet us. And we will know him then for what he was and is. A prince."

The above words were said by the great actor and playwright Ossie Davis at the 1965 funeral of El-Hajj Malik El-Shabaz, better known to the world as Malcolm X. Davis' words were in sharp contrast to the "eulogy" issued by the liberal *New York Times:* "Malcolm X had the ingredients for leadership, but his ruthless and fanatical belief in violence not only set him apart from the responsible leaders of the civil rights movement and the overwhelming majority of Blacks, it also marked him for notoriety and a violent end. Yesterday, someone came out of the darkness that he spawned and killed him."

It was a reflection of the times that Malcolm could be mourned by one America and coldly buried by another. It is a reflection of our present that today he is defined primarily by the halo of iconography that encircles him (not unlike a certain ex-boxer.) Malcolm X stares at us from postage stamps and baseball caps. He is also a staple of "Black History celebrations" once the curt, cold month of February shambles onto the calendar. He is taught as neither shining black prince nor ruthless fanatic but as just another two-dimensional Black leader of the civil rights era. There is a brief mention of his membership in the Nation of Islam, but then, we are quickly assured, as one study guide informs us, he "broke with [the Nation of Islam], rejecting racial separatism" and "continued to speak out until his assassination on February 21, 1965, urging Blacks to take pride in their race and to take action to claim their civil and human rights." Excised from this history is how the man lived.

Born Malcolm Little in 1925 on the edges of Omaha, Nebraska, Malcolm's childhood was defined by racist violence. His father was a Baptist minister and—like Cassius Clay, Sr.—a follower of the Black nationalist leader Marcus Garvey. The family later moved to Lansing, Michigan, where white supremacists torched their home. A racist gang was also believed to be responsible for killing Malcolm's father by shoving him in front of a streetcar. Malcolm's mother became mentally ill under the strain of trying to raise eight children alone and her children were sent to live in foster homes.

Malcolm was a skilled student, but was told by a teacher that his dreams of being a lawyer were "no realistic goal for a nigger." He dropped out, moving to New York and later Boston, where he became a drug dealer and hustler known as Detroit Red, because of the reddish hue in his hair. His life of petty crime ended in 1946 when he went to jail on robbery charges. While in prison, his brother Reginald converted him to the Nation of Islam. Like many Nation of Islam members, he used "X" to stand in for his African name and history eradicated during slavery. Malcolm used the prison's library to complete his education, copying down the encyclopedia and challenging other prisoners to debate. Once released in 1952, he quickly became the Nation's most effective organizer and best-known spokesperson.

Malcolm harshly criticized civil rights leaders for their adherence to nonviolent protest, and their willing ignorance of the problems of Blacks in the North. "They front-paged what I felt about Northern white and Black Freedom Riders going South to 'demonstrate,'" he said. "I called it ridiculous; their own North ghettos, right at home, had enough rats and roaches to kill to keep all of the Freedom Riders busy … The North's liberals have been so long pointing accusing fingers at the South and getting away with it that they have fits when they are exposed as the world's worst hypocrites." These ideas of Malcolm are rarely taught during Black History Month, not surprisingly considering the lack of improvement in many cities since the heyday of the civil rights movement.

Also untaught is Malcolm's derision of the famed 1963 March on Washington as "the farce on Washington," and his criticism of Martin Luther King's advocacy of nonviolence.

Yet Malcolm was frustrated by the inability of the NOI to offer a political alternative to "the farce on Washington." The NOI advocated a strict moral code regarding alcohol, drugs and sexuality and was admired for its anti-racist stance. But it abstained from the civil rights movement and politics generally—restrictions that Malcolm chafed against. "It could be heard increasingly in the Negro communities: 'Those Muslims talk tough, but they never do anything unless somebody bothers Muslims,'" he said later.

The tensions broke into the open after the assassination of President John F. Kennedy in November 1963, described by Malcolm as an example of the "chickens coming home to roost"—a reference to the violence used by the U.S. government at home and around the world, in particular the U.S.-sponsored assassination of Congolese leader Patrice Lumumba and U.S. involvement in South East Asia, in a country few had heard of called Vietnam. Elijah Muhammad used the incident to "silence" Malcolm for 90 days, which led to a permanent break.

At first, Malcolm continued to accept the overall framework of the Nation of Islam. But a trip to Africa and the Middle East accelerated Malcolm's transformation—religiously, into an orthodox

Sunni Muslim, and politically, into a revolutionary who re-conceptualized what had been called the "Negro freedom struggle" as a Black liberation movement bound up with anti-colonial and anti-imperialist struggles worldwide. It was during this time that he changed his name to El-Hajj Malik El-Shabaz.

Just days before his death, Malcolm told a group of Columbia University students that it was "incorrect to classify the revolt of the Negro as simply a racial conflict of Black against white, or as purely an American problem. Rather, we are seeing today a global rebellion of the oppressed against the oppressor, the exploited against the exploiter." In one of his last speeches, he described how imperialism had changed its methods, with the old colonial powers in Asia replaced by the U.S. "They switched from the old, open colonial, imperialistic approach to the benevolent approach," he said. "They came up with some benevolent colonialism, philanthropic colonialism, humanitarianism, or dollarism."

Malcolm's time abroad led him to question his previous political framework. He stopped using the term "Black Nationalist" to describe himself and spoke out in favor of "women's freedom," a break from the Nation of Islam's conservative views. He also changed his speaking and debate style from grim and cutting, to one where he would, as Dick Schaap put it, "Beat you to death with his attractiveness."

Eventually, it was not his "fanaticism" that led to his assassination, but this very attractiveness. Malcolm X was a threat: a threat to both his conservative former allies in the NOI and the United States government. And it is that collective darkness which spawned his assassins; killers who delivered Malcolm to a safer place where he could no longer be so beautifully dangerous.

Defending his heavyweight title

Professional responsibility was quickly thrust upon Ali when he returned to the U.S. to defend his title. Each match became an incredible morality play of the Black Revolution versus the people who opposed it. Ali fought a rematch with Sonny Liston on May 25, 1965, and knocked him out in the first round. Then, in November of that year, he fought Floyd Patterson, a Black ex-champion wrapped tightly in the American flag. Patterson said of his fight with Ali, "This fight is a crusade to reclaim the title from the Black Muslims. As a Catholic I am fighting Clay as a patriotic duty. I am going to return the crown to America." Patterson also called him "a disgrace to boxing and the Negro people." Ali returned fire calling Patterson "The Black White Hope" and saying, "How is he going to return the title to America if I'm from Louisville?"

In the fight itself, Ali brutalized Patterson for all twelve rounds. It was an ugly match. Dundee implored Ali to knock him out, but the champ chose to hold back just enough to humiliate Patterson all the more. Robert Lipsyte described it as watching someone pick the wings off a butterfly. Future Black Panther Party leader Eldridge Cleaver wrote in his 1968 autobiography *Soul on Ice:*

If the Bay of Pigs can be seen as a straight right hand to the psychological jaw of white America, then (Ali/Patterson) was the perfect left hook to the gut.

It is easy to understand why the media and boxing establishment were so furious with Ali for changing his name. It is perhaps harder to understand is why this so galvanized a generation of black freedom fighters, especially as Ali was denouncing integration. Legendary football star and activist Jim Brown spoke to this well when he said. "The nature of the controversy … was that white folks could not stand free black folks. White America could not stand to think that a sports hero that it was allowing to make big dollars would embrace something like the Nation of Islam. But this young man had the courage to stand up like no one else and risk, not only his life, but everything else that he had." Reggie Jackson the famed baseball player, concurred: "Muhammad Ali gave me the gift of self-respect."

It also helped that Ali didn't lose his playfulness as he became more political, a great response to those who said that he would become a "Black Muslim zombie." In typical Ali fashion he jibed:

"I'm not just saying black is best because I'm black. I can prove it. If you want some rich dirt, you look for the black dirt. If you want the best bread, you want the whole wheat rye bread. Costs more money, but it's better for your digestive system. You want the best sugar for cooking; it's the brown sugar."

One writer referred to this as "Ali's ugly period," but for oppressed peoples this was a time of incandescent beauty in the ring and out. As award-winning producer Gil Noble said, "Everybody was plugged into this man, because he was taking on America. There had never been anybody in his position who directly addressed himself to racism. Racism was virulent, but you didn't talk about those things. If you wanted to make it in this country, you had to be quiet, carry yourself in a certain way, and not say anything about what was going on, even though there was a knife sticking in your chest. Well, Ali changed all of that. He just laid it out and talked about racism and slavery and all of that stuff. He put it on the table. And everybody who was black, whether they said it overtly or covertly, said "'AMEN.'"

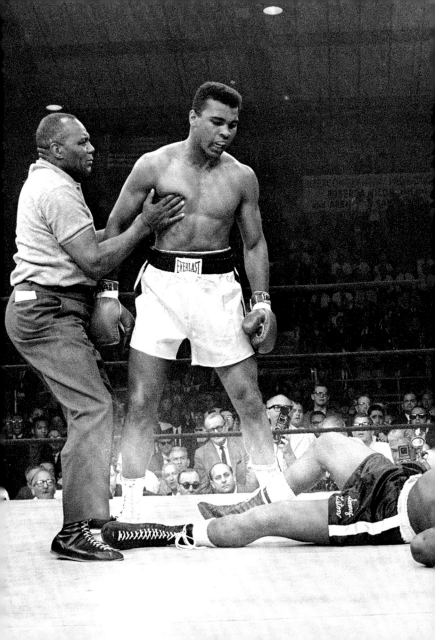

Get up and fight, Sucker!

Previous page: **San Juan, Puerto Rico, August 1, 1965**
Norman Mailer arm-wrestles with Muhammad Ali. Mailer came to watch José Torres, world light heavyweight champion, fight Tom McNeeley. Ali boxed four exhibition rounds after the fight.

Left: **Lewiston, Maine, May 25, 1965**
Referee Joe Walcott restrains Ali as challenger Sonny Liston lies on the canvas after the first round knock down. Ali comfortably retained his world heavyweight title.

Come on, America, come on, white America, say my name. What's my name, fool?

Right: **Las Vegas, Nevada, November 22, 1965**
Floyd Patterson appears groggy as champion Ali whips another sweeping right to his face a moment before their title fight was stopped. Referee Harry Krause stepped in to call it a 12th-round technical knockout.

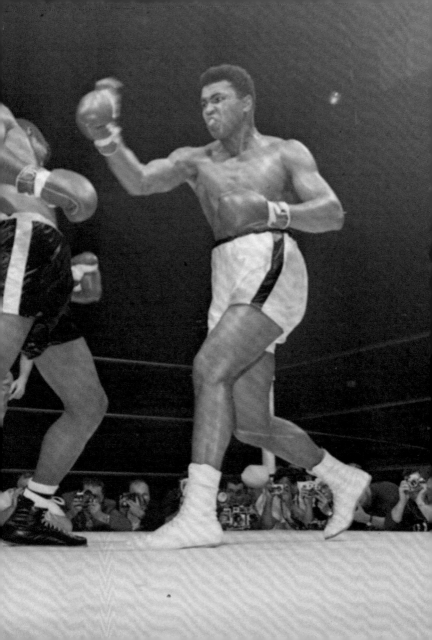

Interview with Eddie Mustafa Muhammad

MARYLAND, 2006

Eddie Mustafa Muhammad is a former World Boxing Association (WBA) Light Heavyweight Champion who retired in 1988 with a lifetime mark of 50-8-1 (39 KO). He trained extensively with Muhammad Ali. Born Eddie Gregory in Brooklyn New York, Eddie Mustafa Muhammad had a reputation for fearlessly taking on all comers. Today Mr. Muhammad is taking on a far bigger foe: the entrenched exploitation of fighters in Professional Boxing. Muhammad is the President and Founder of the Joint Association of Boxing (JAB). Affiliated with the International Brotherhood of Teamsters, JAB is attempting to organize a union in the world of Professional Boxing, and succeeding.

When do you first remember being aware of Muhammad Ali?

I was in junior high school. The first time I heard of Muhammad Ali was when he fought Sonny Liston in Miami. I wasn't into boxing then, but I guess he really pushed me into being a fighter because of the confidence that he had in himself, and the words that he said, and that he backed it up. The fighting was another aspect, but the way he spoke and the way he backed his words up, that had a lot of influence on me because in order for you to say what you're going to do and back it up—that says a lot. That means a lot to me.

Right after the Liston fight, of course, is when he announced he had joined the Nation of Islam and that he was changing his name to Muhammad Ali. What were your thoughts about that at the time?

That right then and there opened up my eyes. He was making clear to the world that he both had his religious principles and believed in himself enough to act upon them in public. So, when he announced that he was going into Islam, I respected that. I already had family that was involved in the Nation of Islam. My older sister and my older brother were already a part of them. So when Ali put his stamp of approval on it, I started doing a lot of reading about being a Muslim in particular.

Being a Muslim, you don't follow Man, you follow what's in the Koran. So it's what's in the Koran that I follow, I don't follow Man. I'm a good listener, I can listen to you all day, but at the end of the day I'm going to follow what's in the Koran. That keeps me balanced both in my personal life and my professional life.

Was it a conflict in your family when your brother and your sister joined the Nation of Islam?

Not at all. They were okay with it because they saw that the religion and the way of life made them and myself more mature and more aware of what they wanted us to be like.

When Ali joined the Nation he was also taking a stand against the integrationist approach of Dr. King and saying that he didn't believe that was possible. A lot of people sympathized with that because they were frustrated with the pace of integration. Was that more militant politics something you were ready to hear at that time?

Know what it is? When people looked at me then, and see in me now—a big Black man with a big, bald head—that's very intimidating to a lot of people. But for me, that has never made me angry or resentful of whites, partly because I've seen more than a few Blacks get intimidated by me also.

I am not a racist. I have never been a racist. If you look up the word "Islam," it means peace. Hating white people is not Islam. That's not in the Koran. When Malcolm X made his Pilgrimage to Mecca, he saw that there were white Muslims that were pure of heart. He slept on the floor with them. He broke bread with them. That opened the door. That opened a lot of minds about the possibilities of brotherhood.

How did you first meet Ali?

A couple of friends of mine out in Newark, New Jersey in the fight game, who were friends of Ali's, would always talk me up to Ali: they said I was an up and coming fighter, and that I was going to be world champion some day. And Ali wanted to meet me. When I was going to fight Marvin Johnson [for the light heavyweight title], that night he came and took me under his wing, opened up his cab door to me, and the story goes on and on. We have a great relationship. We had a great time together.

You trained at Ali's camp. Can you talk about your interaction there?
We used to sit down at either breakfast or dinner and just talk. If it was dinner we talked until the late hours. We would even go horseback riding. It was really a good camaraderie. Just one-on-one, talking and laughing and joking. He had a bus, and he would take everyone who was training at the camp to my fight. In Atlantic City he would drive everybody. It didn't matter who—the cook, everybody. He would bring them to the fight and drive them himself back in the bus. That's support, and that's respect—that man showed me a respect I will never ever forget.

When did you convert to Islam?
I converted to Islam in 1979. I was already familiar with a great deal of the teachings because my older sister and brother had already converted to Islam. I was focused on my boxing. But when Ali asked me to join his camp, which he extended to me for free—let me just say that everything, camp, lodgings, food, use of everything on that camp was at my disposal for free—I saw that he had a mosque in the camp. That tells me a lot about his religion and his way of life. It was no joke. And for me, just being around a person like that: who was very spiritual and then again also a lot of fun, made me commit to being a Muslim. At that camp we talked about life in general and that left a mark on my life that I feel will never go away.

Did you ever pray with Ali after you converted?
We prayed a lot of times. We prayed in New York City. We prayed together with Mike Tyson when Mike got out of prison.

Is it a different experience to pray with Muhammad Ali?

Well, knowing that Ali is a man whose faith is known worldwide, and to be his friend, to laugh and joke, to have fun … and to know that you guys are on the same page, your beliefs are the same is very special.

But it's more of a way of life that we are going to pray. We were in New York a few times, we were in Indiana a few times, we were all over the place—and every time we made time to pray.

We were in Panama one time, and we made the time. And the camaraderie that we had, I remember when he first got his jet plane, he said he wanted to meet me at Newark airport. So, I figured that we were getting ready to go somewhere, and I had to drive all the way to Newark airport. So I stopped by my house, took a quick shower, and when I got to the airport I had to go in the side way where the private jets landed. So I go up to the side and I see a big jet with a butterfly and a bee on the wing. And right away he was telling me "This is my plane and I'm going to fly it," and I said, "You've done lost your mind! If you think I'm getting in there with you flying you're crazy." But I had so much respect and confidence and friendship with him that I got on the plane. But he wasn't flying. He had two pilots that flew the plane. We went to Panama that same day. I didn't even know where we were going. We just jumped in the plane and we were off and running. That's the kind of friendship we had. Wherever the plane landed that's where we'd go.

When is the last time you saw Ali?

The last time I saw Ali was about two years ago. He was out here when Laila [Ali's daughter] was training for a fight. He opened up a gym out here and was at the grand opening. It was good and bad, because I'm not used to seeing him in the situation he's in as far as his health. The Ali I remember [long pause] we used to always joke around and throw punches and he always used to say to me "c'mon, let's go box." That's the Ali I remember.

... I know that he doesn't want us to feel sorry for him. But he is a man that helped me in my career. He extended his hospitality, his courtesy, his everything to boost my career. And it's hard for me to see him in his present condition.

This is a hard question, but do you think he still recognizes you?
Yeah, because there's always that gleam in his eye and that smile on his face. We had so many good times together, that he'll look at me and smile, and you know he recognizes me.
That's got to feel good.
It always feels good when a person of Ali's stature, who was a man of the people, looks at you and gives you that smile like "that's my man."
Can say a little bit about JAB? About why you're involved and what it's mission is?
Well, JAB is something that the fighting establishment needs. The boxers have no voice. Every professional sport has a union so after their playing days are over, they have something to fall back on. They have a pension, they have a medical plan—they have a chance at a life. In boxing, they don't have anything. So, I feel—and not only myself but James Hoffa, general president of the Teamsters—we feel that is what they need. And the good thing about the situation is that when you retire from fighting, we'll have a job waiting for you

with the Teamsters so you can retire with dignity.

Ali famously had a lot of his money taken from him by all manner of hucksters and con artists and disreputable promoters. Do you see JAB as something that could protect boxers from this?

No doubt about it because we will make sure you are not blind about what's going on. You've got to realize one thing: boxing is corrupt. The decisions that are being rendered after the fight—the promotions, the stipulations that are going on—I mean boxing is so corrupt it's unreal! You have a few promoters who are trying to do the right thing for the fighter, but there's only a handful.

Has Ali endorsed your mission in JAB?

He gave us a letter on his stationery saying he supports JAB, and he's all for it. Whatever's for the good of boxing, Ali is for. If this is going to make boxing better, then this is what we need. He endorsed it because of that.

Is there anything else you'd like to say?

I just want to thank Allah for giving me the time spent with a man like Muhammad Ali, because he played a very integral part in my life. Not only as a boxer, but he helped me know a way of life as far as being humble.

I don't care how great you are, nobody's greater than God and on the big stage, you've got to do it right for the betterment of the world, because Islam is a worldly religion. I don't want people going around saying Islam is anything but peace. We have radicals all over the world, different religions, different backgrounds. That's life.

I just want everyone to know that Islam, even though it has a lot of radicals, on the whole, it's a peaceful religion, because this is the way I live my life. I'm not going out there shooting everybody, preaching hate. I love everybody. I have a lot of Jewish friends; I have a lot of Christian friends. I have friends from all walks of life. There's not a hateful bone in my body.

Just like Ali.

Exactly. Islam teaches us that life is too short to hate. The time that you spend trying to hate somebody, turn it into a positive situation. Try to make the world a better place to live. It's like I'm trying to do with JAB. I'm trying to make our sport a better sport, a more respectable sport, to participate in. There are a lot of people who are against it. They want to keep the sport as it is. That way is corrupt. And I'm not trying to have that. I won't have that. I carry Ali with me in my faith and in my mission with JAB.

chapter 4

The wilderness years

Reviled by his country

In 1966 the Army lowered its draft stndards, and in the process reclassified Ali as 1-A—fit for service. The champ was devastated, and began his appeal on March 17, 1966 to be reclassified as a conscientious objector. He claimed that as a preacher for the Nation of Islam, his religion forbade him to fight. The initial judge sided with Ali, but the draft board kept him marked at 1-A, armed with a U.S. Justice Department opinion that Ali's objections to military service were political, not religious. It is hard in retrospect to disagree with the Justice Department, since Ali's "religious" speeches were, reflecting the times, becoming more and more political.

Once again the press was scandalized, as Ali refused to join the sports heroes symbolically "joining" the military. He was called every name in the book, but never bent to the pressure. Instead he fought outside the U.S. On March 29, Ali won a fifteen round decision against Canadian George Chuvalo, and then went to England where he defeated Henry Cooper and Brian London. His next European fight was against the German Karl Mildenberger: it was a difficult contest—Ali finally stopped his opponent in Round 12.

Ali returned to the U.S. in November 1966 to fight Cleveland "Big Cat" Williams in the Houston Astrodome, beating him in three rounds. But his other troubles came to a head on April 28, 1967, when he formally refused induction into the U.S. Army at a recruiting station in Houston, Texas. Student protestors massed outside with a banner that read, "Draft beer not Ali!"

On February 6, 1967, Ali fought an ugly match with Ernie Terrell,

Previous page: **Chicago, February 25, 1966**
Ali addresses a gathering at a Black Muslim convention.

who had enraged Ali by persistently calling him Clay. The champion punished him severely for the insult. Throughout the fight Ali shouted at his opponent "What's my name, Uncle Tom … what's my name?" Terrell endured fifteen rounds of a merciless beating: Tex Maule wrote, "It was a wonderful demonstration of boxing skill and a barbarous display of cruelty." Yet Ali's next contest against Zora Folley on March 22, 1967 saw him at his brilliant best.

On June 20th a jury deliberated 20 minutes before convicting Ali of refusing induction into the Army. He received the maximum sentence: five years in a federal prison and a $10,000 fine, but was freed on bail pending appeal. Howard Cosell commented:

They took away his livelihood because he failed the test of political and social conformity. Nobody said a damn word about the professional football players who dodged the draft, but Ali was different: He was black, and he was boastful.

In August 1967, Ali married Belinda Boyd, a teenage Chicago waitress who worked in a Nation of Islam-owned bakery. She changed her name to Khalilah Ali upon getting married. She was meant to be "the good Muslim wife" Sonji never was.

In early 1968, Khalilah and Muhammad had the first of their four children, Maryum. Instead of going into hiding, he earned money from speaking engagements on college campuses—averaging four a week for the whole year of 1968. The press branded him a coward unwilling to fight for his country, but others agreed with civil rights leader Martin Luther King, Jr: "He is giving up millions of dollars to do what his conscience tells him is right."

Man, I ain't got no quarrel with them Vietcong.

Previous page: **Chicago, February 26, 1966**
Ali wears a uniform of the Black Muslim organization as he attends their convention. He is talking with Sisters of Islam, female members of the group who wear the habit of their order. The newspaper held by Ali carries a photo of Elijah Muhammad, head of the Black Muslims.
Left: **Louisville, Kentucky, March 17, 1966**
Ali pauses on the step to greet a friend, as he arrives at the Veterans building to appeal his 1-A draft classification. Behind him, in dark coat and hat, is his attorney, Edward Jocko.

They maketh me fight out of this country. They leadeth me down the path of bad publicity. I shall be bewailed in the history of sport forever. The sports fan shall follow me all the days of my life.

On being forced to fight George Chuvalo in Canada, as he was refused a license in the U.S.

Right: **Toronto, March 29, 1966**
Challenger George Chuvalo is shown covering up as Ali launches a flurry of punches to his head in the 15th round of their fight. Ali won a unanimous decision.

They can boo me, yell at me and throw peanuts at me—as long as they pay to get in!

Left: **Knightsbridge, London, May 11, 1966**

Ali jogs alongside the Queen's horses taking their morning outing. He was training for his forthcoming title fight with British champion Henry Cooper. The horses were from the Royal Mews, the royal stables at Buckingham Palace.

I am America. I am the part you won't recognize, but get used to me. Black, confident, cocky—my name not yours. My religion, not yours. My goals, my own. Get used to me.

Left: **Lords Cricket Ground, London, May 16, 1965**
World Heavyweight Boxing Champion Muhammad Ali sips a cup of tea at Lords Cricket Ground as he watches the match with West Indies team manager Jeffrey Stollmeyer (left). They are seated on the West Indian dressing room balcony.

You have to give him credit. He put up a fight for one and a half rounds.

On Brian London

Left: **Earls Court, London, August 6, 1966**

Barred from fighting in his own country, Ali traveled to England to fight British hopeful Brian London. He knocked him out in the third round.

I got the height, the reach, the weight, the physique, the speed, the courage, the stamina, and the natural ability that's going to make me great. Putting it another way, to beat me you got to be greater than great.

Left: **Frankfurt, Germany, Sepember 10, 1966**
Karl Mildenberger of Germany hits the canvas after a right from Ali knocks him down in the tenth round of a 15-round title bout. The referee stopped the fight in the twelfth round to save the German from further punishment.

The greatest Ali ever
was as a fighter was
against Williams.
That night, he was
the most devastating
fighter who ever
lived.

Howard Cosell

Right: **The Astrodome, Houston, Texas, November 14, 1966**
Cleveland Williams is spread eagled on the canvas as referee Harry
Kessler sends Ali to a neutral corner.

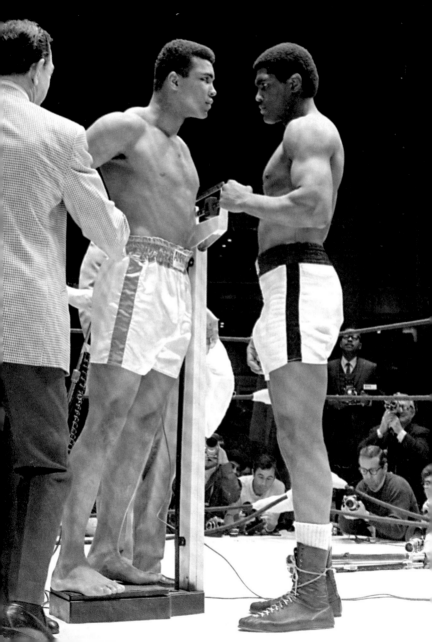

I'm gonna have to be killed before I lose, and I ain't going to die easy.

Left: **Houston, Texas, February 6, 1967**

Ali and Ernie Terrell stare at each other at the weigh-in before their fight. Angelo Dundee gently restrains his fighter as he cocks his arm to match Terrell's clenched fist gesture.

Next page: **Houston, Texas, April 28, 1967**

Ali is escorted from the Armed Forces Examining and Entrance Station by Lt. Col. J. Edwin McKee, commandant of the station, after Ali refused Army induction. Ali faced a possible five-year prison sentence and loss of his title.

He was my first love. He taught me everything I knew, and in the beginning he was beautiful.

Belinda Boyd (Khalilah Ali)

Right: **Chicago, Illinois, August 19, 1967**
Ali with his bride, the former Belinda Boyd, 17, following their marriage at Ali's home. It was the second marriage for Ali. After the marriage, his wife changed her name to Khalilah Ali in accordance with Muslim tradition.

Voices from Congress

Today, other than throwing out the first pitch at a baseball game, there is nowhere a member of the political establishment would rather be than posing next to Muhammad Ali. Politicians of all stripes adore the prospect of basking in his glow. It speaks strongly to the amazing journey Ali has traveled. Ali biographer Thomas Hauser researched comments by members of congress in the mid-1960s. Their words are a reminder of just how incendiary Ali was, something unmentioned when George W. Bush gave him the Presidential Medal of Freedom in 2005.

Frank Clark (PA):
The heavyweight champion of the world turns my stomach. I am not a superpatriot. But I feel that each man, if he really is a man, owes to his country a willingness to protect it and serve it in time of need. From this standpoint, the heavyweight champion has been a complete and total disgrace. I urge the citizens of this nation as whole to boycott any of his performances. To leave these theater seats empty would be the finest tribute possible to that boy whose hearse may pass by the open doors of the theater on Main Street USA.

Peter Thompson (GA):
I take the floor today to protest the network that has announced it will use Cassius Clay as a commentator for

these contests. I consider this an affront to loyal Americans everywhere, although it will obviously receive much applause in some of the hippie circles. Maybe the American Broadcasting System feels that it needs to appeal more to the hippies and yippies of America than loyal Americans.

Robert Michel (IL):
Clay has been stripped of his heavyweight title for dodging the draft. And I consider it an insult to patriotic Americans everywhere to permit his reentry into the respected ranks of boxing. It should be recalled that Mr. Clay gave as one of his excuses for not wanting to be drafted that he is in reality a minister and that even boxing is antagonistic to his religion. But apparently he is willing to fight anyone but the Vietcong. ... I read with disgust today the article in the Washington Post concerning the upcoming fight of this country's most famous draft dodger, Cassius Clay. The article said that Mr. Clay was out of shape, overweight, and winded. No doubt, this comes from his desperate and concerted efforts to stay out of the military service while thousands of patriotic young men are fighting and dying in Vietnam. Apparently, Mr. Clay feels himself entitled to the full protection of the law, yet does not feel he has to sacrifice anything to preserve the institutions that protect him. Cassius Clay cannot hold a candle to the average American boy who is willing to defend his country in perilous times.

John Rarick (LA):
Veterans who have fought our nation's wars feel that any man unwilling to fight for his country is unworthy of making a profit or receiving public acclaim in it. Cassius Clay is a convicted draft dodger sentenced to a five-year prison term which he is not serving. What right has he to claim the privilege of appearing in a boxing match to be nationally televised? The Clay affair approaches a crisis in national indignation.

William Nichols (AL):
The United States Supreme Court has given another black eye to the United States Armed Forces. The decision overturning the draft evasion conviction of Cassius Clay is a stinging rebuke to the 240,000 Americans still serving in Vietnam and the 50,000 Americans who lost their lives there. I wish that the members of the Supreme Court would assist me when I try to explain to a father why his son must serve in Vietnam or when I attempt to console a widow or the parents of a young man who has died in a war that Cassius Clay was exempted from.

Joe Waggoner (LA):
The United States Supreme Court has issued the edict that

Cassius Clay does not have to be inducted because he does not believe in war. No draft-age young man believes in a war that he will have to fight, nor does any parent of a draft-age son believe in a war that their own flesh and blood will have to fight and possibly give his life in so doing. But our people have always heeded the call of their country when asked, not because they love war, but because their country has asked them to do so. And I feel strongly about this. If Cassius Clay does not have to be drafted because of questionable religious beliefs or punished for refusing induction simply because he is black or because he is a prizefighter—and I can see no other real justification for the Court's action—then all other young men who wish it should also be allowed a draft exemption. Cassius Clay is a phony. He knows it, the Supreme Court knows it, and everyone else knows it.

The white race attacks black people. They don't ask what's our religion, what's our belief? They just start whupping heads. They don't ask you, are you Catholic, are you a Baptist, are you a Black Muslim, are you a Martin Luther King follower, are you with Whitney Young? They just go whop, whop, whop!

Right: **University of Notre Dame, Indiana, May 20, 1968**
Ali addresses students in the old field house at the University.

Ali's campus speeches

By 1968, Ali was out on bail, abandoned by the Nation of Islam and hangers-on, and stripped of his title. But he was never more active because there was a young generation of Blacks and whites that wanted to hear what he had to say. "The onliest boxer anyone ever talked to like a senator" obliged. In 1968, he spoke at 200 campuses, includng the Ivy leagues, Black Colleges, and Penitentiary programs. Ali discussed this "year of the speeches" with Thomas Hauser. "Putting the lectures together was hard work. I had six of them, and first I wrote out all my ideas on paper. Then I wrote them again on note cards, studied them every day, and practiced giving speeches in front of a mirror with Belinda listening. Sometimes I tape recorded it so I could hear myself and learn how to improve what I said. I did that for about three months until I was ready, and the first speeches turned out good. Talking is a whole lot easier than fighting. I must have gone to two hundred colleges, and I enjoyed the speaking. It made me happy."

Ali's lectures were an interesting study in cross-cultural communication. He would speak against marijuana smoking and interracial dating, with an old fashioned tone that would make some of the New Lefties in attendance wince. As Robert Lipsyte said, "Ali was providing a window on a lot of social, political, and religious things that were going on in America; a window into the black world that wouldn't have been available to most of his listeners any other way." But as the year went on, the eminently intuitive Ali found his voice and connected with his audience politically. Typically, he would start quietly, telling his audience, "As most of you know, I'm no longer in boxing, so I accept college invitations to come out and meet you." But soon, he'd be shouting, "Can my title be taken away without me being whupped?" "No!" the audience would thunder.

"One more time!"

"No!"

"Now I'd like to hear this from you, and I want the world to hear. Who's the heavyweight champion of the world?"

"You are."

"One more time. We don't want no excuses. They might say the film was bad or the camera was broke. Who's the champ of the world?"

"You are!"

Here is a sampling of Ali speeches from 1968:

On the war in Vietnam: "I'm expected to go overseas to help free people in South Vietnam, and at the same time my people here are being brutalized and mistreated, and this is really the same thing that's happening over in Vietnam. So I'm going to fight it legally, and if I lose, I'm just going to jail. Whatever the punishment, whatever the persecution is for standing up for my beliefs, even if it means facing machine-gun fire that day, I'll face it before denouncing Elijah Muhammad and the religion of Islam."

On being stripped of his title and denied the right to fight: "The power structure seems to want to starve me out. The punishment, five years in jail, ten-thousand-dollar fine, ain't enough. They want to stop me from working, not only in this country but out of it. Not even a license to fight an exhibition for charity, and that's in this twentieth century. You read about these things in the dictatorship countries, where a man don't go along with this or that and he is completely not allowed to work or to earn a decent living."

On the financial hardship he was enduring: "What do I need money for? I don't spend no money. Don't drink, don't smoke, don't go nowhere, don't go running with women. I take my wife out and we eat ice cream. My wife is such a good cook I never go to a restaurant.

I give her twenty dollars for a whole week and it's enough for her. We can eat on three dollars a day. Look out there at that little robin pecking and eating. The Lord feeds the birds and the animals. If the Lord has this power, will the Lord let His servant starve, let a man who is doing His work go hungry? I'm not worried. The Lord will provide."

On integration and segregation: "Why ask me if I believe in segregation. I recognize the fact that you believe in it. What do you mean, you don't believe in it? Oh, man, you're just crazy. Every city I go to, I can find a black neighborhood and a white neighborhood. How many Negroes live out here in this big old neighborhood? I'd like to see peace on earth, and if integrating would bring it, I'd say let's integrate. But let's not just stand still where one man holds another in bondage and deprives him of freedom, justice, and equality, neither giving him his freedom or letting him go to his own."

On lack of black pride: "We've been brainwashed. Everything good is supposed to be white. We look at Jesus, and we see a white with blond hair and blue eyes. We look at all the angels; we see white with blond hair and blue eyes. Now, I'm sure there's a heaven in the sky and colored folks die and go to heaven. Where are the colored angels? They must be in the kitchen preparing milk and honey. We look at Miss America, we see white. We look at Miss World, we see white. We look at Miss Universe, we see white. Even Tarzan, the king of the jungle in black Africa, he's white. White Owl cigars. White Swan soap, White Cloud tissue paper, White Rain hair rinse, White Tornado floor wax. All the good cowboys ride the white horses and wear white hats. Angel food cake is the white cake, but the devils food cake is chocolate. When are we going to wake up as a people and end the lie that white is better than black?"

On the need for a separate black homeland: "We were brought here four hundred years ago for a job. Why don't we get out and build our own nation and quit begging for jobs? We want a country. Why can't I have my own land? Why can't I build me a house? Why can't we be free? We've been down so long we can't even imagine having our own country. You know, we're forty million people. We're the wisest black people on the planet; we learn everything the white man knows. Black people from Africa come here, learn half of what we know, and they go home and run their own country. We'll never be free until we own our own land. We're forty million people, and we don't have two acres that's truly ours."

On hate: "I don't hate nobody and I ain't lynched nobody. We Muslims don't hate the white man. It's like we don't hate a tiger; but we know that a tiger's nature is not compatible with people's nature since tigers love to eat people. So we don't want to live with tigers. It's the same with the white man."

On money versus principle: "I could make millions if I led my people the wrong way, to something I know is wrong. So now I have to make a decision. Step into a billion dollars and denounce my people or step into poverty and teach them the truth. Damn the money. Damn the heavyweight championship. I will die before I sell out my people for the white man's money. The wealth of America and the friendship of all the people who support the war would be nothing if I'm not content internally and if I'm not in accord with the will of Almighty Allah."

It was pretty bad.
But I was great.

Left: **New York City, December 2, 1969**
Ali wears a beard and wig for his acting debut in the Broadway musical
"Buck White."

Surviving the ban

Three and a half years. That's how much time Muhammad Ali lost at his physical peak, exiled for refusing to fight in a war millions in the United States were beginning to oppose. During his time away, Ali eked out a living on the campus lecture circuit, Broadway and even in a staged computer-generated bout against retired champ Rocky Marciano. The "computer" (or those programming it) determined that the smaller, slower Marciano would have beaten Ali—in the stateside version. When they released it to the world— miraculously—Ali was the victor. This is called "niche marketing."

As this mock "battle of the ages" was put together, Marciano told Ali's wife Belinda, "Tell Muhammad to stop torturing himself. Get him out of boxing, and forget the whole thing." It was sage advice from a retired champion who left the fight game undefeated with his mind intact. But Ali's debts were snowballing. His handlers attempted, even as Ali faced a Supreme Court prison sentence, to find him a venue to ply his trade. Because his passport had already been seized, in an echo of an earlier African-American leader, Paul Robeson, Ali had to stay in-country and walk, hat in hand, as one state boxing commission after another denied him a license to fight. He came very close to securing a deal in California, but the governor, a man named Ronald Reagan said, according to Harold Conrad, "That draft dodger will never fight in my state, period."

Yet Ali, more and more, began to get a hearing among ordinary people in the U.S. because of several interrelated factors. The first and most critical was that the country was turning against the war in Vietnam. Demonstrations were mushrooming in size, and the nation was divided. This, along with Ali's years in exile, changed the perception of him among some from a "draft-dodger" to a man of foresight and principle. As fight guru Jim Jacobs said, "The exile from boxing was the best thing that could have happened to Ali. In terms of his skills, it was a tragedy. But in terms of his earning power, it was a plus … It showed people that Ali was sincere. It made him an underdog."

Ali was finally issued a license to fight, after three and a half years, by the state of Georgia. The state was still run by an arch segregationist governor named Lester Maddox. But it was also home to Atlanta, the birthplace of Dr. Martin Luther King, and a resurgent liberalism. It was also one of the few places without an unaccountable, corrupt state fight commission. Ali's return was negotiated directly with Atlanta Mayor Sam Massell, a Jew, and an African-American state senator named Leroy Johnson. Maddox grumbled but, in a telling view of the tenor of the times, did not stand in the way.

Ali's opponent was to be a young puncher named Jerry Quarry, and the fight was set for February 6, 1967. In the pre-fight press conference Ali made clear that he understood the significance of his return. "I'm not just fighting one man," he said:

I'm fighting a lot of men, showing them here is one man they couldn't conquer. Lose this one, and it won't be just a loss to me. So many millions of faces throughout the world will be sad; they'll feel like they've been defeated. If I lose, for the rest of my life I won't be free. I'll have to listen to all this about how I was a bum, how I joined the wrong movement and they mislead me. I'm fighting for my freedom.

The sooner this country does away with the draft, the better off we'll be.

Dr. Martin Luther King

Left: **Houston, Texas, March 29, 1967**
Ali confers with Black Civil Rights leader Dr. Martin Luther King. Ali was in Houston for his court suit to prevent his Army induction. The court refused to block his call-up.

Ali's stand against the Vietnam war

Some of the best minds in the United States believed that a war in Vietnam was in the best interests of humanity. A boxer thought they were wrong. Muhammad Ali's journey from hated member of a Black Nationalist sect, to anti-war lightning rod, is the stuff of legend. It is also the most dangerous part of his history because it speaks most strongly to the issues of imperial war and principled resistance that mark our present as much as our past.

In early 1966, President Lyndon Johnson called for a massive expansion of the draft. Suddenly the need for hundreds of thousands of ground troops in S.E. Asia became official foreign policy. To satisfy this need, the passing percentile in the Army intelligence test was lowered from 30 to 15, making Ali just eligible for service. He heard this news surrounded by reporters and he blurted out one of the most famous phrases of the decade: "Man, I ain't got no quarrel with them Vietcong." Bang! That was the headline. The media exploded.

This was an astounding statement. There was little opposition to the war at the time. The antiwar movement was in its infancy and most of the country was in favor of conquering S.E. Asia. As Mike Marqusee has noted, "The cover of *Life* magazine's cover read, 'Vietnam the War is Worth Winning.' The number one song the 'Ballad of the Green Berets' was climbing the charts. And then there was Ali."

Ali was no anti-war prophet. He was someone truly bewildered that his life could take such a drastic turn. "For two years the army told everyone I was a nut and I was ashamed. And now they decide I am a wise man," he said. "Now, without ever testing me to see if I am wiser or worser than before, they decide I can go into the army

… I can't understand it, out of all the baseball players, all of the football players, all of the basketball players—why seek out me, the world's only heavyweight champion?" He was asking questions that deserved examination. But the reaction in the press was immediate, hostile, ferocious and at times amusingly hysterical. His nemesis Jimmy Cannon wrote,

"He fits in with the famous singers no one can hear and the punks riding motorcycles and Batman and the boys with their long dirty hair and the girls with the unwashed look and the college kids dancing naked at secret proms and the revolt of students who get a check from Dad, and the painters who copy the labels off soup cans and surf bums who refuse to work and the whole pampered cult of the bored young."

Sportswriter Murray Robinson was prescient when he wrote, "For his stomach-turning performance, boxing should throw Clay out on his inflated head. The adult brat, who has boasted ad nauseam of his fighting skill but who squealed like a cornered rat when tapped for the Army should be shorn of his title. And to the devil with the old cliché that a ring title can be won or lost only in the ring." The two most famous sportswriters in the United States weighed in strongly against Ali. Red Smith declared, "Cassius makes himself as sorry a spectacle as those unwashed punks who picket and demonstrate against the war." In the *Los Angeles Times,* Jim Murray called the champ "the white man's burden."

Jack Olsen wrote years later in *Sports Illustrated:* "The noise became a din, the drumbeats of a holy war. TV and radio commentators, little old ladies … bookmakers, and parish priests, armchair strategists at the Pentagon and politicians all over the place joined in a crescendo of get Cassius get Cassius get

Cassius." Ali was given every opportunity to recant, to apologize, to sign up on some cushy USO gig boxing for the troops and the cameras, just like Joe Louis did during World War II. But he refused. As Ali explained to the Louisville draft board:

"Sir, I said earlier and I'd like to again make that plain, it would be no trouble for me to go into the Armed Services, boxing exhibitions in Vietnam or traveling the country at the expense of the Government or living the easy life and not having to get out in the mud and fight and shoot. If it wasn't against my conscience to do it, I would easily do it. I wouldn't raise all this court stuff and I wouldn't go through all of this and lose the millions that I gave up and my image with the American public that I would say is completely dead and ruined because of us in here now. I wouldn't jeopardize my life walking the streets of the South and all of America with no bodyguard if I wasn't sincere in every bit of what the Holy *Qur'an* and the teachings of the honorable Elijah Muhammad tell us and it is that we are not to participate in wars on the side of nonbelievers, and this is a Christian country and this is not a Muslim country."

His refusal was gargantuan because of what was bubbling over in U.S. society. There was the Black revolution over here and the draft resistance and antiwar struggle over there. And there was the heavyweight champ with one foot planted in both.

Dave Kindred, the veteran sportswriter, captured this dynamic when he wrote, "You had riots in the streets; you had assassinations; you had the war in Vietnam. It was a violent, turbulent, almost indecipherable time in America, and Ali was in all of those fires at once, in addition to being heavyweight champion of the world." An incredible groundswell of support built up for Ali. That is why, despite the harassment and the media attacks and prospects of a prolonged stay in a federal prison, he stood firm.

At one press conference later that year, he was expected to apologize. Instead he stood up and said, "Keep asking me, no matter how long, on the war in Vietnam, I sing this song, I ain't got no quarrel with the Vietcong."

As poet Sonia Sánchez remembered, "It's hard now to relay the emotion of that time. This was still a time when hardly any well-known people were resisting the draft. It was a war that was disproportionately killing young Black brothers and here was this beautiful, funny poetical young man standing up and saying no! Imagine it for a moment! The heavyweight champion, a magical man, taking his fight out of the ring and into the arena of politics and standing firm. The message was sent."

But Sánchez and her compatriots were still a minority view. No less a force than army veteran and sports trailblazer Jackie Robinson said, "He's hurting the morale of a lot of young Negro soldiers over in Vietnam. And the tragedy to me is, Cassius has made millions of dollars off of the American public, and now he's not willing to show his appreciation to a country that's giving him, in my view, a fantastic opportunity. That hurts a great number of people."

On March 29, 1966 the Kentucky State Senate passed a resolution condemning Ali. "His attitude," the resolution read, "brings discredit to all loyal Kentuckians and to the names of the thousands who gave their lives for this country during his lifetime."

Jerry Izenberg, another young writer willing to listen to Ali, remembered, "I can't tell you what I went through for defending him. All the cancellations of my newspaper column, the smashed car windows, the bomb threats; the thousands of letters from Army war veterans talking about Jews like me and concentration camps." By becoming such a polarizing political figure, he became someone everyone, love him or hate him, had to see.

Right on, brother!

Ali said years later "All kinds of people came to see me. Women came because I was saying, 'I'm so pretty', and they wanted to look at me. Some white people, they got tired of my bragging. They thought I was arrogant and talked too much, so they came to see someone give the nigger a whuppin'. Longhaired hippies came to my fights because I wouldn't go to Vietnam. And black people, the ones with sense, they were saying, 'Right on, brother; show them honkies.' Everyone in the whole country was talking about me."

In 1967 Martin Luther King, Jr. came out against the war, another huge step for the antiwar movement. In a press conference King explained his opposition: "Like Muhammad Ali puts it, we are all—Black and Brown and poor—victims of the same system of oppression." Ali and King, to the anger of the NOI, struck up a private friendship that we know about thanks to the good people at the FBI. Here is one short wire-tapped transcript with Martin Luther King, Jr. in which Muhammad Ali is referred to derisively as "C."

"MLK spoke to C, they exchanged greetings. C invited MLK to be his guest at the next championship fight. MLK said he would like to attend. C said he is keeping up with MLK and MLK is his brother and he's with him 100 percent but can't take any chances, and that MLK should take care of himself and should 'watch out for them whities.'"

The only time these private friends came together in public was later in 1970, when Ali joined King in Louisville, where a bitter and violent struggle was being waged for fair housing. Ali spoke to the protesters saying, "In your struggle for freedom, justice and equality I am with you. I came to Louisville because I could not remain silent while my own people, many I grew up with, many I went to school with, many my blood relatives, were being beaten, stomped and kicked in the streets simply because they want freedom, and justice and equality in housing." Ali then cemented his position as a lightning rod between the freedom struggle and the antiwar struggle when a reporter kept dogging him about the war, until finally he turned around, cameras whirring and said:

Why should they ask me to put on a uniform and go 10,000 miles from home and drop bombs and bullets on Brown people in Vietnam while so-called Negro people in Louisville are treated like dogs and denied simple human rights? No I'm not going 10,000 miles from home to help murder and burn another poor nation simply to continue the domination of white slave masters of the darker people the world over. This is the day when such evils must come to an end. I have been warned that to take such a stand would cost me millions of dollars. But I have said it once and I will say it again. The real enemy of my people is here. I will not disgrace my religion, my people or myself by becoming a tool to enslave those who are fighting for their own justice, freedom and equality ... If I thought the war was going to bring freedom and equality to 22 million of my people they wouldn't have to draft me, I'd join tomorrow. I have nothing to lose by standing up for my beliefs. So I'll go to jail, so what? We've been in jail for 400 years.

It was an outrage; an absolute disgrace ... Why? How could they? There'd been no grand jury impanelment, no arraignment. Due process of law hadn't even begun, yet they took away his livelihood because he failed the test of political and social conformity, and it took him seven years to get his title back. It's disgusting. To this day, I get furious when I think about it.

Howard Cosell

Left: **Induction Center, Houston, Texas, April 28, 1967**

Ali is interviewed by the veteran sports commentator Howard Cosell, who holds an ABC microphone. Cosell was a social crusader and firm supporter of Ali, both as boxer and political activist. When Ali embraced the Muslim faith and changed his name, only Cosell would honor it by calling him Ali during interviews. Cosell's interviews with the boxer were masterpieces in entertainment—the two men became an iconic double act in their own right.

A man of conscience

It was still in the air whether Ali would step forward when his name was called at the induction center in Texas. When the officer called for "Cassius Clay," he did not move. He was told that he was risking fine and imprisonment by refusing induction. He said he understood.

Afterward he made clear just how much he understood. "I am proud of the title 'World Heavyweight Champion', which I won in the ring in Miami on February 25, 1964. The holder of it should at all times have the courage of his convictions and carry out those convictions, not only in the ring but throughout all phases of his life. It is in light of my own personal convictions that I take my stand in rejecting the call to be inducted into the armed services. I do so with full realization of its implications and possible consequences. I have searched my conscience, and I find I cannot be true to my belief in my religion by accepting such a call. My decision is a private and individual one. In taking it I am dependent solely upon Allah as the final judge of these actions brought about by my own conscience. I strongly object to the fact that so many newspapers have given the American public and the world the impression that I have only two alternatives in this stand—either I go to jail or go to the Army. There is another alternative, and that alternative is justice. If justice prevails, if my constitutional rights are upheld, I will be forced to go neither to the Army nor jail. In the end, I am confident that justice will come my way, for the truth must eventually prevail."

Years later Ali said he had no regrets. "Some people thought I was a hero. Some people said that what I did was wrong. But everything I did was according to my conscience. I wasn't trying to be a leader. I just wanted to be free. And I made a stand all people, not just black people, should have thought about making, because it wasn't just black people being drafted. The government had a system where the rich man's son went to college, and the poor man's son went to war. Then, after the rich man's son got out of college, he did other things to keep him out of the Army until he was too old to be drafted."

One hour after Ali refused induction—before he'd been charged with any crime, let alone convicted—the New York State Athletic Commission suspended his boxing license and withdrew recognition of him as champion. Soon, all other jurisdictions in the U.S. followed suit, and the title Ali had worked for throughout his life was gone. It was the beginning of his three-and-a-half-year exile from the ring.

Ali's refusal to cross the line was front page news, not only in America, but around the world. In Guyana, Cheddi Jagan led a picket of the U.S. embassy. In Karachi, a young Pakistani fasted outside the U.S. consulate. There was a demonstration in Cairo.

An editorial in the *Ghana Pioneer* deplored what it called the "concerted efforts" to strip Ali of his championship. During the first major British demonstration against the war in April 1967, among the host of leaflets handed out in Grosvenor Square was one reading, "LBJ Don't Send Muhammad Ali to War." Bertrand Russell congratulated Ali on his courage and assured him, "The air will change. I sense it." Ali at this point saw himself as someone who had a responsibility to an international base of support.

Boxing is nothing, just satisfying to some bloodthirsty people. I'm no longer a Cassius Clay, a Negro from Kentucky. I belong to the world, the black world. I'll always have a home in Pakistan, in Algeria, in Ethiopia. This is more than money.

Support also began to come from unlikely sources at home. Floyd Patterson, who was himself being shaped by the movements around him said, "What bothers me is Clay is being made to pay too stiff a penalty for doing what is right. The prize fighter in America is not supposed to shoot off his mouth about politics, particularly if his views oppose the government's and might influence many among the working class that follows boxing."

The day of Ali's conviction the U.S. congress voted 337-29 to extend the draft four more years. They also voted 385-19 to make it a federal crime to desecrate the flag. At this time, 1,000 Vietnamese noncombatants were being killed each week by U.S. forces. One hundred soldiers were dying every day, the war cost $2 billion a month and the movement against the war was growing.

As Julian Bond said, "When Ali refused to take that symbolic step forward everyone knew about it moments later. You could hear people talking about it on street corners. It was on everybody's lips. People who had never thought about the war—Black and white— began to think it through because of Ali. The ripples were enormous."

Right: **London, April 2, 1970**
John Lennon and Yoko Ono give their shorn hair to Abdul Malik, British Black Muslim leader, who presents them with a pair of Muhammad Ali's boxing shorts. The hair was auctioned to the highest bidder to fund the anti-Vietnam war effort.

The return of the Black Prince

All the great names of the black establishment were at ringside for Ali's crucial return bout against Jerry Quarry. The young Rev. Jesse Jackson said: "If he loses tonight, it will mean, symbolically, that the forces of blind patriotism are right, that dissent is wrong, that protest means you don't love the country. This fight is Love-it-or-leave-it vs. Love-it-or-change-it. They tried to railroad him. They refused to accept his testimony about his religious convictions. They took away his right to practice his profession. They tried to break him in body and in mind. Martin Luther King used to say 'Truth crushed to the earth will rise again.' That's the black ethos. And it's happening here in Georgia of all places, and against a white man."

Before the fight even started it was clear how much had changed in the 1,000 days Ali had been away from the ring. African-Americans were no longer content to be on the back of the bus. They arrived at the fight in confident droves. In addition, reforms and jobs programs won by the civil rights movement had expanded the Black middle class. Black was beautiful, and Muhammad Ali was considered the great pioneer of this concept, the one who showed the world and Black America that this was fact.

Bert Sugar recalled, "It was probably the greatest collection of black power and black money ever assembled up until that time. Bill Cosby, Sidney Poitier, Jesse Jackson, Julian Bond, Ralph Abernathy, Andrew Young, Coretta Scott King, Whitney Young. People were arriving in hand-painted limousines, dressed in colors and styles I'd never seen. They'd come for the return of Muhammad Ali, and there was no doubt in their mind that he'd win. They weren't boxing fans; they were idolaters … it was *Gone With The Wind* turned upside down."

Julian Bond echoed Sugar's amazement at the crowd. "The whole audience was composed of stars; legitimate stars, underworld stars. You had all these people from the fast lane who were there, and the style of dress was fantastic. Men in ankle-length fur coats; women wearing smiles and pearls and not much else. Then the fight started. I was sitting behind this youngish blond woman, and all through it I kept hitting her on the back in my excitement. And she was so excited, she never turned around and told me to stop. All I can remember saying is, 'Stick him, Ali! Stick him! Stick him!' It was more than a fight, and it was an important moment for Atlanta, because that night, Atlanta came into its own as the black political capital of America."

New York Times writer Robert Lipsyte said to me:

It was the true victory of Black Power. This was Black Power—a Black state senator. This guy had been in exile for three and a half years. All that meant—here's no Federal body of boxing—was that every single boxing commissioner—city, state, all around America, and his passport had been pulled so he couldn't fight overseas—refused to sanction a fight. The title had been stripped already. Nobody would let him fight in America, except the city of the new South, the City That's Too Busy to Hate. He made it happen … So what could this be but true Black Power? And the return of the Dark Prince in exile? It was an enormously symbolic event.

But none of this would have meant anything if Ali had lost the fight. And he certainly won handily, with a TKO in the third round against the overmatched Quarry. But it was clear to the veteran fight watchers that this was a different fighter after three and half years of exile. Gone with the wind was the man so quick, you couldn't lay a glove on him.

As his fight doctor Freddie Pacheco said, "When Ali went into exile, he lost his legs. Before that, he'd been so fast, you couldn't catch him, so he'd never taken punches. He'd been knocked down by Henry Cooper and Sonny Banks, but the truth is, he rarely got hit and he'd never taken a beating. In the gym, he'd work with Luis Rodríguez, who was the fastest welterweight in the world; and Luis, who was like lightning, couldn't hit him … [Ali] discovered something which was both very good and very bad. Very bad in that it led to the physical damage he suffered later in his career; very good in that it eventually got him back the championship. He discovered he could take a punch."

Left: **Atlanta, Georgia, October 26, 1970**
Ali hits a hard right to Jerry Quarry in his long-awaited return to the ring. The fight was stopped after the third round and Ali was declared the winner.

Next page: **Atlanta, Georgia, October 26, 1970**
Ali receives congratulations from Dr. Ralph Abernathy, president of the Southern Christian Leadership Conference, and Mrs. Coretta King, widow of slain civil rights leader, Dr. Martin Luther King, after Ali's defeat of Jerry Quarry. Mrs. King presented Ali with the Martin Luther King Sports Medallion.

Interview with Dave Kindred
MARYLAND, MAY 2006

Dave Kindred, sportswriter for *The Washington Post, The Atlanta Journal-Constitution,* **and** *The Sporting News,* **among other publications, is the author of the best-selling book** *Sound and Fury,* **which explores the relationship between sports commenator Howard Cosell and Ali.**

Your book on the Cosell/Ali relationship is called Sound and Fury. How did you come up with that?

Actually I didn't choose the title. The editor of the book did. I quickly agreed because first of all, there's a lyricism to it. A friend of mine said "You're stealing from Faulkner." And I said "Well, he stole from Shakespeare. I only steal from the best." Sound and Fury was perfect. I thought the picture that my publisher ran on the cover with Cosell under "Sound" and Ali under "Fury" was perfect, because that's the way people think of them, and yet at the same time it works both ways. It connects to the epigraph that I chose from Edith Wharton, who said, "There are two sources of light,/The candle,/And the mirror that reflects it." Both guys work both ways, the sound and the fury, the candle and the mirror.

What attracted Cosell to the idea of being a champion of Ali at that point in the mid-1960s, when so many journalists were turning their back on him, and he was such a reviled figure?

First of all they had a relationship before he became Ali. When Ali was still known as Cassius Clay, Cosell was a local New York radio/television broadcaster working for the ABC station in New York. He met Clay in 1962 when Clay was 21 years old and just a kid having fun. Cosell was this obsessively ambitious guy—he had announced to at least one guy that he was going to be the most famous broadcaster in America. Clay was making noise about being the youngest world heavyweight champion ever and was predicting the round that he knocked people out in, with poetry and laughs and getting all the attention in the sports world at that time. Cosell saw that. I think he decided then, "This is a kid to pay attention to" and, consciously or unconsciously, decided to hitch his wagon to that star. So when Clay in 1964 announced that he had joined the Nation of Islam and taken the name Muhammad Ali—and with the early indications that he was going to refuse the draft—he became a reviled figure. People refusing the draft were fleeing to Canada, to Sweden, and were generally thought to be un-American.

So here was the world heavyweight champion, perhaps the most famous athlete in the world, refusing induction into a war that people in the U.S. thought was important. So for Cosell to stand with him was an act of principle. At the same time, it was an act of expediency. ABC at the time was the "Almost Broadcasting Company." In a three-network world, ABC was so far down the totem pole as to be number four or number five. So anything that brought attention to ABC was good. And certainly Ali became their property. NBC and CBS had no reason to want Ali. Their sports departments were small and did nothing to put on games. ABC under Roone Arledge created "Wide World of Sports," a new concept in sports programming that could be called journalism. And they used Ali for that. Cosell and Ali, by appearing together so many times on ABC, helped raise the network's profile. So Cosell, while at heart a social crusader, was at heart also a very ambitious guy. Ali's fame and Ali's infamy worked for Cosell because he wanted to stand with him on the social issues and he certainly wanted to ride with him to fame.

You also write in the book about Cosell's experience with anti-Semitism growing up. Do you think that had any impact on his affinity for Ali?
I think it had everything to do with it. They were different people in almost every way, from age to geography to social class to religion to race. And yet at bottom, the thing they had in common was far more powerful than those superficial things. They had in common a sense of oppression, a sense of being an underdog, a sense of being unappreciated, even oppressed on account of race and religion. Cosell grew up in what he described as an anti-Semitic kind of atmosphere in Brooklyn. He recalled several times being chased by kids from St. Theresa's Parish, of being taunted by phrases such as "Jesus killer."

His daughter Jill said to me that her father's entire life was shaped by one thought: that he was a poor Jewish boy. Even at the height of his fame, the height of his wealth, that he still at bottom considered himself a poor Jewish boy. I think he saw in Ali's persecution a mirror, a reflection of his own perceived persecution. And certainly in Cosell's life, it was probably more obvious: the bias, the bigotry, the prejudice against Cosell as a Jewish broadcaster was probably more palpable than any racism that affected Ali. Cosell had it much harder to get where he got. Cosell was 36 years old before he became a broadcaster, 52 years old before he was on "Monday Night Football." It was a long, what he thought, hard climb and he always saw anti-Semitic enemies lurking. So I think he had that kind of feeling, whether real or perceived, of persecution on the matter of his religion, on the matter of his culture—he was not a religious guy, but certainly he was a Jewish guy. I think that sense of persecution, he felt, almost made him a kindred spirit, if you will, with Ali, who he saw as being persecuted unfairly through the mid-Sixties.

Why did Jerry Izenberg call Cosell "the Black man's white man"? I ask that question because, to me, it means for Cosell it was about more than just Ali, but a broader sense of social justice.

Cosell was, at bottom, always a social crusader. Before he became a broadcaster, he worked as a lawyer. He became friends with Jackie Robinson, because he had grown up as a Dodgers fan. So he knew Robinson in the late Forties and early Fifties. As a lawyer he represented Willie Mays and Monte Irvin when they couldn't get representation otherwise. The Izenberg line about "the Black man's white man" came after they did a documentary—Izenberg was the writer and producer—on the [historically Black] Grambling College football team.

Grambling didn't turn out as many professional football players as Notre Dame, say, but certainly many more than most big-time universities, and yet no one knew anything about them. So Izenberg, who really had a greater social conscience than Cosell, proposed doing a documentary. This was a time when Cosell was off the network but looking for a way on, so he started producing documentaries. And the first one that Izenberg and Cosell did together was on Grambling. For *A Hundred Yards to Glory,* Izenberg went down to Grambling to film the show, and in Izenberg's mind the success of that show gave Cosell the bona fides as the "Black man's white man," because no one had ever done a network documentary on Grambling College football, let alone a white man from Brooklyn.

Do you think Ali, or people around Ali, were aware of that reputation? I don't think so. I never found anything, ever, that showed Ali ever had an introspective thought about Cosell. Ali was not a deep thinker in any way. All he knew was that Cosell welcomed him on national television and that was enough for him. The rest of it, I never saw any evidence that Ali knew anything about Cosell's reputation, other than the way Cosell treated him.

One of the most interesting parts of your book is when you speak about them as a comedy team. Can you talk a little about why you even took that tack of looking at it, and what you found out talking to experts on comedy teams?

They were on television so many times, in so many ways, that they developed a *shtick*, they developed pieces of business that, if you watched enough video tape, read enough about them you saw things that kept appearing, such as the "truculent" line.

They used the "truculent" line many times, where Ali would be popping off and Cosell would be agitating him, and Ali would get huffy, and Cosell would say, "Muhammad, you're being very truculent today." And Ali would say "Whatever 'truculent' means, if that's good, that's what I am." And they knew what worked on television, they knew the roles that they were playing, so it occurred to me that this was a comedy team. Edwin Pope, one of the newspaper people that I interviewed, called them the "Abbott and Costello of sports."

So when you look at it, when you see enough of it, you see the way they look at each other, you see the way they stand with each other, you see the way that Cosell smiles as he starts to ask a question, because he knows what he's doing and what Ali's answer is going to be. I talked to a professor named Lawrence Epstein who did a history of comedy teams. He told me Cosell and Ali were their own sight gag. When you look at Ali, tall and handsome, a shining golden child standing alongside this homely guy from Brooklyn with the obvious toupee. There was the difference in their voices—Ali almost like a Baptist preacher, Cosell with that nasal Brooklyn whine. Everything about them was such a contrast that it worked to be funny without even hearing what they were saying.

That's so interesting because you talk about their contrasts, yet you have this line in the book that I loved "One was beauty and one was beast, and we never knew which was which." Most people would say Ali was the beauty and Cosell was the beast. Clearly, you see beauty in Cosell, and sometimes something less than beautiful in Ali. Can you speak about that?

That goes back to what you said in the beginning about *Sound and Fury.* Sound and fury, the candle and the mirror, beauty and the beast. I detailed several times in the book behavior from Ali that I think is contemptible. It wasn't new. There was nothing new in any of it, from his abandonment, almost betrayal, of Malcolm X in 1964 through his continued association with low-life con men into the 90s. The way that he disparaged Joe Frazier before each of their three fights. Before the first fight he said that only the Ku Klux Klan is rooting for Joe Frazier, somehow turning Joe Frazier into the white guy in this fight. That was all contemptible.

But there is "beauty" in Cosell?

I think there is, because certainly Cosell had an effect on me at an early age, before I ever heard his voice. Cosell used to write a column in the back of *Sport Magazine* in the late Fifties, early Sixties called "Speaking of Sports." It was always basically a story. It wasn't a real opinion piece. It was a story about the great characters and performers in sports. I was always interested more in the people in sports than I am in the Xs and Os or who's going to win, and that's what Cosell was interested in. So from the start I was ready to like Cosell, and as I became a columnist Cosell was rising in fame and always had opinions. And his opinions generally matched mine. We tend to like those people who think like us, so it seemed to me that Cosell was always on the right side of every question. And to me there was a beauty in that.

He was a social commentator as much as he was a sports broadcaster, and certainly that was the kind of sports journalism that I wanted to practice. He always talked about how he wanted to do something important, run for the Senate, be the ABC Evening News anchor. Well, I thought what he did was important. And I believe that he knew it was important, or he wouldn't have kept doing it. He certainly had all the money that he could have needed. He had all the influence he could have needed. He could have just quit sports broadcasting and become an anchor somewhere if he wanted to and work his way to wherever he wanted to be. I think what he did was important. He showed that sports journalism mattered, certainly, and he always said that "SportsBeat," the magazine show that he did for about three years at the end of his career, was the most important work that he'd ever done—with some self-justification in that, because certainly no one remembers "SportsBeat." But it was significant that he said that, because that's the way he thought of himself. That's the sports broadcaster he wanted to be. Instead he got caught up in the fame of "Monday Night Football."

Do you think Monday Night Football was when he crossed the line from journalist to shtick?

He became a parody of himself. From the start, he didn't like it. He liked the fame, he liked the attention, he certainly liked the money, but it was not the kind of thing that really was at his heart. He was much more of a performer there. There was no doubt that he liked the performance aspect of it. So it's not as if he was doing it with a gun to his head. He liked being on the television shows, the Partridge Family, the Odd Couple, the Woody Allen movies that he did. But it was different, this Cosell of the 1970s. It was not the Cosell of the 60s, it was not the Cosell of the late 80s. It was a Cosell that I, basically, could do without. The Cosell that rose to great fame in the 70s was the least of the Cosells that I liked.

Who was the Cosell of the late 80s?

The one that did "SportsBeat." He did "SportsBeat" in the early 1980s but it ended when he wrote the third book, *I Never Played the Game* where he excoriated all the ABC people, and the show was almost immediately cancelled. Ratings were miserable, anyway, so it ended then. That was the Cosell I admired, because he and his people in that show were doing real-world stories about sports. It wasn't just glorification, it wasn't just reporting, it wasn't just performance, they were real stories about real issues. It's the progenitor of "Real Sports" with Bryant

Gumbel. What Gumbel does is what Cosell was doing twenty years ago. They're doing it better now, there's no doubt about that in terms of production, but Cosell was the originator.

What happened to the relationship with Ali and Cosell?

The strapline of the book—where it says "Two Powerful Lives, One Fateful Friendship"—the word "friendship" is an overstatement. It was always a working partnership. It became a friendship when they both were offstage, in the mid- to late Eighties, when Ali was retired, Cosell was off network television. When they met, they were very warm to each other and knew that they had made a grand adventure together so they became much more friendly then. Before that, they had so little in common; just the TV stuff was basically their relationship. Cosell always admired and respected him, but it was not as if they went to dinner together, or went on family trips together, or anything like that, they were not that kind of friends.

You have a quote from Cosell where he says, "Arrogant, pompous, obnoxious, vain, persecuting, distasteful, verbose, a showoff. I have been called all of these and, of course, I am." Was there more to him?

The thing that many people don't understand, is that Cosell was much more Cosell off the air than he was on the air. Off the air, in a hotel lobby, you couldn't escape him. He was a show. He wanted to be a show. He was much more obnoxious off the air than he was on the air. Drinking had a lot to do with that. He was a big drinker. Everybody I talked to said they never saw him drunk. Maybe it was one of those cases where they never saw him sober.

Do you think that, in today's sports landscape, there is room for someone to be able to talk about social commentary through sports?

I think there is. I certainly do it as often as I can. To ignore it is to ignore an important part of the culture. I still work a lot from Robert Lipsyte's book *Sports World*. I think what sports does is reflect what's going on in America, and I think if you don't talk about it, you're failing your responsibility as somebody who's been given a forum. It's not just fun and games. The games can be fun. But the games are important in what they teach us about the way we live in this country at this time.

Doesn't that make Ali truly special? For all your criticisms of him, many of which I think are valid, doesn't it make him special in that when he really had to be 12 feet tall, he was; and that he took these unpopular positions that in some respect have been proven correct by history?

That's a good question. Ferdie Pacheco says in his book that Ali did all these things for what he—Pacheco—believes were the wrong reasons, and they all turned out right. He talked about "Ali's luck." You could make the case for Ali almost any way you want to make it because, there's enough evidence on everything, and Ali himself provided most of this conflicting evidence. You can make the case that he refused the draft, it was the principled thing to do and it turned out to be the right thing to do, but he did it because he was ordered to do it. But so what if he were ordered, you might say? If Billy Graham, to choose another religious leader, orders me not to go to war, is that any different than Elijah Muhammad ordering Ali not to go to war? I'm not sure you can diminish Ali's act because he was simply following Elijah Muhammad's order; he still did it, and he was still the one who was going to go to jail. He was still willing to go to jail and never wavered from that. I talked to Ann Braden, a famous civil rights worker in Louisville, and she said "I don't care why he didn't go. He didn't go, and that was important to us, meaning people involved in the anti-war struggle. Just the fact that this most famous person in the world is not going—we don't care why he's not going. Just like we don't care how people get AIDS, we just need to help them. We don't care why Ali didn't go, he inspired us. His example inspired us. David Halberstam has written that Ali was perhaps the only person of fame that gave up anything to protest Vietnam. He gave up the championship, he gave up the three and a half greatest years of any athlete's life, and, at least seven times by my count, was only one legal decision away from going to prison for five years. Yet he never wavered in his commitment to his stand. I couldn't ever find one time where he did. In fact Izenberg asked him in Canada, "You're thinking about going to Canada?" and he said "No, this is my country. I'm going to stay." He never made the slightest effort at evading the consequences of that decision.

Elijah Muhammad also took a step back from him when his title was stripped, giving him more reason to cave and he still didn't.

Elijah Muhammad read him out of the Nation, and effectively stripped him of his name. "You will be Cassius Clay. You are no longer Muhammad Ali. You are no longer welcome." Who knows why that was done? Elijah claimed it was done because Ali wasn't professing enough faith in Allah to provide, because when he went on the air with Cosell he said that he needed money, he needed a fight, he needed money. It was expedient for Elijah, too, because Ali wasn't making money any more; all he was doing was bringing more opprobrium down on the Nation by being this uppity draft-dodger. He was no longer useful, and as soon as he became useful again Herbert Muhammad was right there with him, and Elijah, all that stuff just went away.

You were in Louisville in the early Sixties. What kind of town was it?

I really had no idea. I was 24 years old, my first job, coming from a town of 1300 people. I was just trying to get by. Until 1970, all of my copy in the *Louisville Courier-Journal* referred to Ali as Cassius Clay. He became Muhammad Ali in 1964, but his hometown newspaper still referred to him as Cassius Clay six years later. So that had to be reflective of the town's thinking. Probably today, still, even with the Muhammad Ali Center, still, I'd bet a great majority of the people of Louisville despise him.

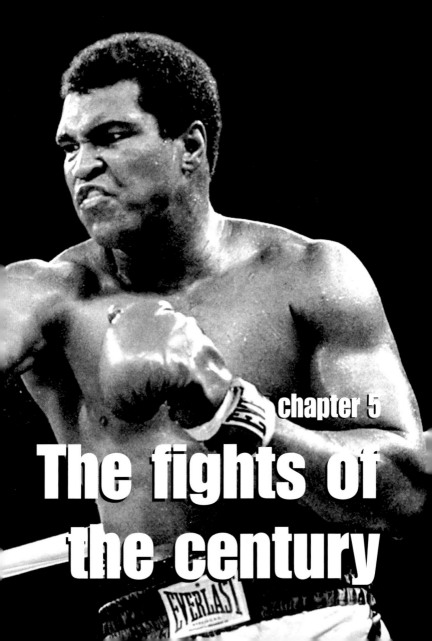

chapter 5

The fights of the century

Ali's epic era: 1971–75

When Ali defeated Jerry Quarry in Atlanta in 1970, it was obvious that he was a very different fighter from the one who had been suspended in 1967. He was slower, cagier, and more willing to take a punch. The boxer who was too fast to be hit discovered—much to his surprise—that he had the toughest chin in perhaps the history of the sport. That chin would serve him well on March 8, 1971 when he finally met Joe Frazier at Madison Square Garden. After Ali was stripped of his title, it had gone to Frazier: that's why Ali called him "the fake champion."

This was to be the first modern boxing extravaganza, with each boxer splitting an unheard of $5 million in what was called "The Fight of the Century." Incensed by Ali's taunt of "Uncle Tom," Frazier inflicted the first defeat of Ali's career—a 15-round decision capped by knocking his opponent down in the 15th round with a brutal left hook. Frazier then spent three weeks in a hospital and Ali, humbled in defeat, and covered by a new generation of sportswriters, finally began to receive some positive press.

Ali's fortunes then began to change. On June 28, 1971 the U.S. Supreme Court unanimously reversed the four year old draft evasion conviction, saying that his claim to be a conscientious objector was based on religion and was sincere. Its decision, it was readily obvious, was due far more to the power of the civil rights movement and the changing mood in the country about the war in Vietnam than to the facts of the case. One judge expressed the hope that the decision "would give black people a lift."

Following Joe Frazier's stunning defeat of Ali, the lives of the two men seemed headed in opposite directions. Frazier was the now undisputed champion. A child of poverty from Jim Crow South

Carolina, he was invited to speak before his state's legislature, the first time an African-American had been so asked in forty years. He was a hero to the Southern establishment because he had vanquished the insidious, draft dodging Black Muslim.

Yet, in part because he accepted offers like this, Frazier was never quite able to diminish Ali in the mind of the public at-large. As one commentator put it:

I guess Joe had an unrealistic expectation of what would happen after he beat Ali. He thought all of the Ali-related problems that existed in his mind, particularly in terms of acceptance by the black community, would go away. And they didn't. Joe still wasn't perceived as the total champion, and he blamed that entirely on Ali.

Previous page: **Manila, Philippines, October 1, 1975**
Heavyweight champion Muhammad Ali connects with a right in the ninth round of "The Thrilla in Manila"—his famed title fight with Joe Frazier.
Next page: **Miami Beach, Florida, February 9, 1971**
Heavyweight champion Muhammad Ali, his father Cassius Clay, Sr., and his brother Rahaman Ali, together at Ali's training camp.

Frazier-Ali: the fight of the century

On March 8, 1971 Muhammad Ali took on Joe Frazier in a historic encounter. It pitted two unbeaten fighters against each other—Frazier the nominal champion vs. Ali the people's champion. But the back-story, the personalities and conflicts, transcended the fight.

Smokin' Joe Frazier, a 1964 Olympic Gold Medallist, was one of 14 children from Beaufort, South Carolina. Unlike Ali who grew up in a stable home, Frazier came from the "underclass" and punched his way out of a life of abject poverty and degradation. During Ali's exile Frazier lent Ali money, and appeared with him in public to help keep him in the public eye by continuing his speaking agreements. Joe had no problem with Ali's decision not to serve in the Army saying, "If Baptists weren't allowed to fight, I wouldn't fight either." Frazier even went to a couple of meetings of the Nation of Islam, out of respect for Ali more than anything else. In return Ali gave Frazier support and, some would say, generous cover, by recognizing him as the champion. But in the lead up to the fight, the contest—vamped up by Ali—became constellated around what made them different. As one observer wrote:

It was a classic match-up between boxer and slugger … It was Ali the draft-dodger versus patriotic Joe; Ali the loudmouth versus softspoken Joe; Ali the Muslim against honest Bible-reading Baptist Joe … But most of all, the fight was becoming 'uppity' versus 'conformist' black—the fact that Joe Frazier was, if anything, more typical of black America than Ali.

Of course there was the typical good-natured Ali clowning. He uncorked this classic poem:

> Joe's gonna come out smokin'
> But I ain't gonna be jokin'
> I'll be pickin' and pokin'
> Pouring water on his smokin'
> This might shock and amaze ya
> But I'm gonna destroy Joe Frazier.

Ali also said, "Fifteen referees. I want fifteen referees to be at this fight because there ain't no one man who can keep up with the pace I'm gonna set except me. There's not a man alive who can whup me. I'm too fast. I'm too smart. I'm too pretty. I should be a postage stamp. That's the only way I'll ever get licked."

But Ali also fed on the polarization in the United States saying:

Any black person who's for Joe Frazier is a traitor.... The only people rooting for Joe Frazier are white people in suits, Alabama sheriffs, and members of the Ku Klux Klan. I'm fighting for the little man in the ghetto.

There may have been some truth in this. As Bryant Gumbel said, " if Ali lost, it was as though everything I believed in was wrong … After a while, how you stood on Ali became a political and generational litmus test. He was somebody we could hold on to; somebody who was ours. And fairly or unfairly, because he was opposing Ali, Joe Frazier became the symbol of our oppressors."

Ali, in shameful fashion also called Frazier a "gorilla" and preyed on his insecurities about his intelligence and appearance. Joe Frazier still reflected this twenty years later saying, "[T]he words hurt me more than the punches. Now he says he did it to help our gate, but the gate didn't have nothing to do with it … Calling me an Uncle Tom; calling me the white man's champion … Ali wasn't no leader of black people. He didn't lead me, except when I was running. Doing roadwork, I'd set him up in my mind on the road in front of me and go four miles saying, 'I'm gonna catch you, Cassius Clay' … A lot of people went to the fight that night to see Clay's head knocked off, and I did my best to oblige them."

The fight went down in history. It was also uniquely brutal. The dean of boxing referees Arthur Mercante said:

Ali and Joe did a lot of damage to each other that night. Both of their faces were misshapen afterward. Ali's face was no longer round. Frazier's was all bruised, swollen, and cut up.

The clincher came in the 15th round when Frazier floored Ali with a crushing left hook. The shot hit Ali so squarely several ringside observers swore they saw his face begin to swell before he hit the floor.

But in a greater surprise than the punch was Ali's response. Arthur Mercante recalled: "[Ali] went down, and anyone else would have stayed on the canvas, but he was up in three seconds."

But resilience did not sway the judges and Frazier was the victor by unanimous decision. Much of the press relished Frazier's victory. "If they fought a dozen times," wrote Red Smith, "Joe Frazier would whip Muhammad Ali a dozen times; and it would get easier as they went along." But Gumbel reflected the other side saying. "And when Ali lost, I was devastated. It was awful." Ali commented:

Against Frazier, I knew he'd be tough. He was harder for me than Liston or Foreman, because he had what I was vulnerable to—a good in-close left hook ... If I was young, I'd have danced for fifteen rounds, and Joe wouldn't have ever caught me. But the first time we fought, I was three-and-a-half years out of shape. He punched hard; he pressured me good ... But it would be wrong to say I gave the fight to Joe. I didn't give it away. He earned it.

But when he heard that Frazier said he would never want a rematch, Ali merely smiled and said, "Oh, how wrong he is."

It was billed simply as "The Fight." Both men were guaranteed 2 and half million dollars each which at the time was the biggest payday in history. Anyone who was anyone was there. Even Frank Sinatra was ringside taking photographs.

Boxing journalist Lee Bellfield

Left: **Madison Square Garden, New York, March 8, 1971**
A famous moment during the Fight of the Century—the Ali-Joe Frazier heavyweight title bout. Movie star Frank Sinatra—himself surrounded by photographers—sizes up a shot. Unable to acquire a ringside seat, Sinatra got himself commissioned by *Life* magazine to ensure a prime position.

Next page: **Madison Square Garden, New York, March 8, 1971**
Joe Frazier is directed to the ropes by referee Arthur Marcante after knocking Ali down during the 15th round of the title bout. Frazier won on points.

Just lost a fight, that's all. There are more important things to worry about in life. Probably be a better man for it. News don't last long. Plane crash, ninety people die, it's not news a day after. My losing's not so important as ninety people dying. Presidents get assassinated, civil rights leaders get assassinated. The world goes on. You'll all be writing about something else soon. I had my day. You lose, you don't shoot yourself.

Left: **New York, March 10, 1971**
Ali at the wheel of his van before leaving New York. The night before he had been defeated by Joe Frazier in a 15-round decision.

Making up for lost time

With the Fight of the Century behind him, Ali's luck changed and his conviction was overturned by the Supreme Court. The "Louisville Lip" was uncharacteristically quiet and pensive, realizing that he would not have to spend half a decade in a federal pen.

It's like a man's been in chains all his life, and suddenly the chains are taken off.... He don't realize he's free until he gets the circulation back in his arms and legs and starts to move his fingers. I don't really think I'm going to know how that feels until I start to travel, go to foreign countries, see those strange people on the street. Then I'm gonna know I'm free.

Now that jail was in the rear view, Ali started fighting like he was making up for lost time—but he was also absorbing tremendous punishment. This became most apparent on March 31, 1973 when he suffered a shocking defeat by Ken Norton, in a 12-round decision. Norton was a journeyman fighter but he was in phenomenal shape. The match drew tremendous attention. As Howard Cosell said, "So many of Ali's fights had incredible symbolism, and here it was again. Ken Norton, a former Marine, in the ring against the draft-dodger in San Diego, a conservative naval town. Richard Nixon had just been re-elected with a huge mandate. Construction workers were marching through the streets supporting the war in Vietnam, which showed no signs of winding down."

The self-image that Ali seemed to project so effortlessly even affected the mindset of the in-ring professionals there to look after his well being. Ali's jaw was broken badly early in the fight, "shattered" as one observer put it. His fight doctor Ferdie Pacheco, considered throwing in the towel but said in retrospect, "Everything had to do with Muslims and Vietnam and civil rights, and if Ali lost, it was more than a fight. So you didn't just have a white guy say 'Stop the fight', especially if Ali didn't want it stopped.

On September 10, 1973 Ali barely won an ugly rematch with Norton and then on January 28, 1974 he avenged his defeat of Joe Frazier, winning a 12-round decision. On October 30, 1974, Ali fought the heavily favored Foreman in Kinshasa, Zaire, with the fighters splitting a $10 million purse. Flamboyant promoter Don King famously called the fight "The Rumble in the Jungle".

Ali bragged in the lead up about how he would use his speed, but in the fight itself, he lounged against the ropes, letting the champ punch himself into exhaustion. This was called his "rope-a-dope." He scored an eighth-round knockout as the crowd cheered, "Ali boma ye!" ("Ali kill him!") Don King saw the adulation and attached himself to Ali for the rest of his career.

Ali's public transformation was complete when Elijah Muhammad died on February 25, 1975. His son Wallace took over the Nation of Islam, preaching a less strident message than his father's. Eventually Ali declared, "Wallace taught us the true meaning of the Koran. He showed us that color doesn't matter."

At home I am a nice guy—but I don't want the world to know. Humble people, I've found, don't get very far.

Right: **Chicago, Ilinois, June 28, 1971**
Ali and his wife take a stroll near their home in Chicago.

Next page: **Houston, Texas, July 27, 1971**
Ali drives a left to the jaw of Jimmy Ellis in the 12th round of their fight. Ali scored a technical knockout in this round after driving Ellis into the ropes with repeated blows to the face and body.

Everybody knows me and knows I am the champion.

Left: **Las Vegas, June 27, 1972**
Ali protests that he is the heavyweight champion of the world after he was introduced as the former champion at the weigh-in ceremony for his match against Jerry Quarry.

That's what these fights are about: literally, a guy going out and keeping his head above water. He fought Jerry Quarry three weeks before Dublin, which says it all. For him, it was like going to the ATM machine and getting another 200 grand.

Irish columnist Dave Hannigan

Right: **Dublin, Ireland, July 11, 1972**
Ali is interviewed in Dublin a week before his upcoming fight against Al "Blue" Lewis.
Next page: **Dublin, Ireland, July 18, 1972**
Ali has a lighthearted sparring match with American film director John Huston just before his 12-round bout against Lewis.

This fight against a game ex-convict from Detroit marked the culmination of an extraordinary week in Ireland's sporting and cultural history. From the moment the world's most charismatic athlete touched down at Dublin Airport and announced his maternal great-grandfather Abe Grady had emigrated from County Clare more than a century before, the country was in his thrall and, of course—being Ali—he loved it.

Read Ireland news

Left: **Croke Park Stadium, Dublin, July 19, 1972**
Ali slams a left hook into Al "Blue" Lewis during a 12-round fight. Ali won in the 11th round when the referee stopped the fight.
Next page: **West Point, New York, August 7, 1972**
Ali, in typical teasing mode, toys with the toupee of ABC television sports commentator Howard Cosell.

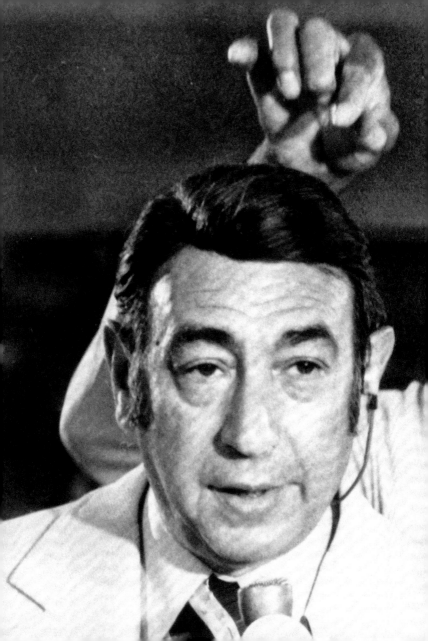

Of all the men I fought ... Floyd Patterson was the most skilled as a boxer.

Left: Deer Lake, Pennsylvania, 1972

Floyd Patterson works out on a punching bag while Ali peeks in the open window. Ali has invited Patterson to help him formally dedicate his new training camp and work out there for a day. The two heavyweights would face each other in a 12-round bout in New York on 20th September. Ali won by a knockout in the seventh round.

A Prize fight is like a war: the real part is won or lost somewhere far away from witnesses, behind the lines, in the gym, and out there on the road long before I dance under those lights.

Right: **Stateline, Nevada, November 21, 1972**
Ali jogs along a snow-covered road.

250

Will they ever have another fighter who writes poems, predicts rounds, beats everybody, makes people laugh, makes people cry, and is as tall and extra pretty as me?

Left: **Las Vegas, Nevada, February 14, 1973**
Britain's Joe Bugner takes a right-hand smash from Ali in the 10th round of their heavyweight fight. Ali won the contest by decision.

> # When we told Ali his jaw was probably broken, he said, 'I don't want it stopped.'... And still, he fought the whole twelve rounds.

Ali's fight doctor Ferdie Pacheco

Right: **San Diego, California, March 31, 1973**
Ken Norton pounds into Ali who has backed into the corner during their 12-round heavyweight bout. Norton won on a split decision.

Ali and Belinda seem to be true soulmates whose marriage is strengthened by their faith.

Review author Rusty White

Left: **Deer Lake, Pensylvania, August 21, 1973**
Ali's wife Khalilah (formerly Belinda) sits surrounded by their children at Ali's training camp where he is preparing for his re-match with Ken Norton. Muhammad Jr. is in Khalilah's lap and Maryum is standing behind her. Twins Reesheda (left) and Jamillah (right) are at her side.

I took a nobody and created a monster. I put him on the dating game. I gave him glory. Now I have to punish him bad.

Right: **Inglewood, California, September 10, 1973**
Ali crashes a right to the side of Ken Norton's head during a middle round of their 12-round re-match, which Ali won by decision.

Next page: **Madison Square Garden, New York, January 28, 1974**
Ali throws a punch at Joe Frazier, right, during their 12-round bout. He won the fight by decision.

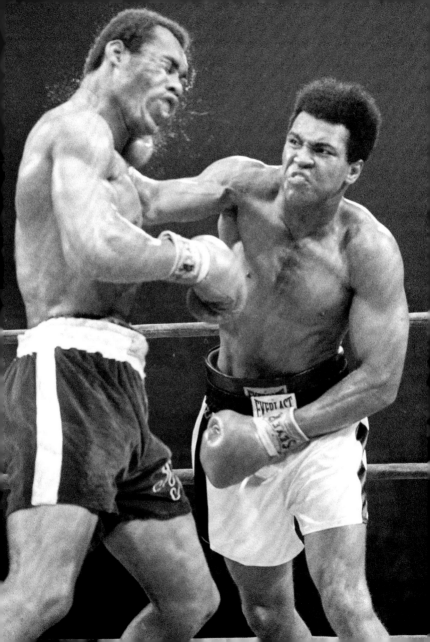

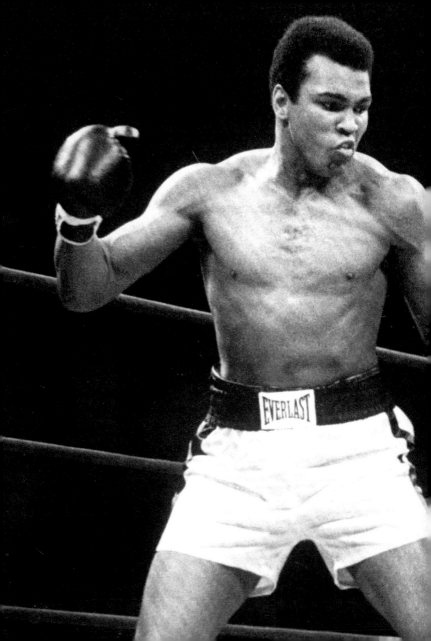

The Rumble in the Jungle

**If you think the world was shocked when Nixon resigned
Just wait 'till I whup George Foreman's behind!**

So said Muhammad Ali as he prepared for the biggest challenge of his career taking on the young, mountainous George Foreman in Zaire. Never has a fight been so fraught with symbolic weight. The simplistic model as put forward by promoter Don King, was that this was "The Rumble in the Jungle," two American Olympic gold medalists, going back to "the motherland" to fight for the title; "from the slave ship to the championship" as King said with his typical huckster's bombast. For the press, the fight held the potential to be a sad folly. Ali was seen as a fading figure, 34 years old, twice defeated. Foreman, who had dispatched Frazier with such methodical ferocity, would punch Ali into retirement.

The symbolic value took on a greater meaning when seen through the eyes of Africa. In the Global South Ali was a hero of transcendent importance. As Congolese artist Malik Bowens remembered, "We knew Ali more for his political stance. The United States was in war [Vietnam] against a Third World country and one young man said, 'You want me to fight your war? No.' He may have lost his title and millions of dollars but that is where he won the esteem of millions of Africans …his skin was lighter than ours, but it wouldn't matter how white he was because of what he stood for … he was defending the good cause for the whole world." Ali further endeared himself to his host continent saying, "Damn America! Damn what America thinks! Because I'm going to Africa to fight among my brothers!" He was at his loquacious best, saying,

"It's a great feeling being in a country operated by black people. I wish all black people in America could see this. In America, we've been led to believe that we can't do without the white man, and all we know about Africa is jungles. All we see of Africa is a bunch of natives leading white men on a safari, and maybe one of the white men is trapped by a gorilla and the natives save him. We never get shown African cars and African boats and African jet planes. They never tell us about the African TV stations. And everything here is black. The soldiers, the president, the faces on the money. It don't seem possible, but twenty-eight million people run this country, and not one white man is involved. I used to think Africans were savages. But now that I'm here, I've learned that many Africans are wiser than we are. They speak English and two or three more languages. Ain't that something? We in America are the savages."

That didn't mean the mischievous Ali always stepped perfectly. At one point he said: "All you boys who don't take me seriously, who think George Foreman is gonna whup me; when you get to Africa, Mobutu's people are gonna put you in a pot, cook you, and eat you." A representative from the Zairian government sent a missive to Ali saying, "Please tell Mr. Ali that we are not cannibals; we don't eat people. We're doing the fight to create trade and help our country, and Mr. Ali's remarks are damaging our image."

George Foreman, meanwhile, arrived in Africa with a German shepherd; a poor choice considering the shepherd was the dog of choice for Zaire's colonial occupiers, the Belgians. As one local asked, "Why does he come to our country with the dogs with which they attacked us?" Foreman, who today has an unerring sense of public relations having built an empire on the basis of his sparkling personality, was moody and withdrawn, seeming about as thrilled to be in Africa as the recipient of a root canal.

I'm gonna fight for the prestige, not for me, but to uplift my little brothers who are sleeping on concrete floors today in America. Black people who are living on welfare, black people who can't eat, black people who don't know no knowledge of themselves, black people who don't have no future.

Left: **Kinshasa, Zaire, September 17, 1974**
Ali is cheered by admirers as he drives through downtown Kinshasa for a sightseeing trip. Ali was in Zaire to face George Foreman for their epic "Rumble in the Jungle" fight.

The bout was meant to be a celebration of the emerging Black Power, with Don King as lead promoter and an All Star Kinshasa concert featuring "Soul Brother Number One" James Brown joining African artists Miriam Makeba in a celebration of Pan-African glory. This didn't thrill the old guard of writers at all. "They're holding the world heavyweight championship fight in the Congo," groused Jim Murray of the *Los Angeles Times*. "I guess the top of Mount Everest was busy. I don't know why they can't hold it in Yankee Stadium like everybody else."

But Murray knew why. This was about making plain the changes that had rocked the world over the last decade. A billboard erected between the airport and the Zaire capital of Kinshasa blared, "Zaire, Where Black Power is a Reality." The sign, it was later reported, was erected to block squatter camps from the arriving media. Zaire existed under the iron first of Dictator Mobutu Sese Seko—a darling of the U.S. who had been party to the CIA sponsored killing of Malcolm X's old friend Patrice Lumumba. Ironically, Lumumba was the international symbol of Pan-Africanism, his murder a symbol of the power the West. After seizing power, true to form, Mobutu looted a quarter of the country's wealth. In the lead up to the fight, Mobutu rounded up scores of alleged criminals and had 100 of them executed in order to ensure calm for the foreign press and dignitaries.

As Norman Mailer said, "Most dictators are unbelievably ugly or plain. His picture was everywhere." Ali and Foreman got a taste of life under Mobutu when Foreman suffered a cut in training and the fight was delayed. Rumors swirled that the fight would possibly be cancelled or moved, but Mobutu made perfectly clear that everyone was staying. But if everything surrounding the fight was smeared with the ugly politics of the cold war, the fight itself approached legend. Foreman was considered unbeatable. His professional record was forty wins and no losses, with thirty-seven knockouts. Howard Cosell delivered a choked up monologue in the weeks leading up to the "Rumble", begging Ali not to take the fight. Ali mocked Cosell's concern saying, "Howard! You say I'm not the man I was ten years ago. Well, I talked to your wife and she says you're not the man you were two years ago! Cosell! That hair on your head is phony and it comes from the tail of a pony!" But his joking couldn't mask what the press was seeing with their own eyes. Observers gaped slack-jawed in amazement when Foreman would punish his heavy bag with brutal roundhouse shots, caving them in like John Henry wielding his hammer.

Again, Ali laughed it off. "When Dick Sadler [Foreman's trainer] holds the heavy bag, George can punch a hole through it. But when we get in the ring, ain't nobody gonna be holding me. No one hits me with seven or eight punches in a row like George hit Joe Frazier. And George telegraphs his punches. Look out; here comes the left. Whomp! Here comes the right. Whomp! Get ready, here comes another left. Whomp! I'm not scared of George. George ain't all that tough. What you white reporters got to remember is, black folks ain't afraid of black folks the way white folks are afraid of black folks."

Ali would say to everyone who would listen, "I'm going to be dancin'! I'm gonna dance! I never seen George tired yet, huffing and puffing, get winded and have to take a few punches. And when George gets tired, I'll still be dancing. I'll be picking my shots, beating him at will. If George Foreman don't get me in seven, I'm telling you now, his parachute won't open." While it thrilled the hearts of his supporters to think that Ali was too fast to catch, once again reality told a different story. The 32-year-old Ali didn't have the legs he once had.

The postponed fight was rescheduled for 4:00 A.M. on October 30. "Before Ali fought Joe Frazier," Wali Muhammad would say later, "we thought he just couldn't lose. But we were wrong, and against Foreman we were worried. George had been built up to be such a great fighter. People thought he'd kill Ali. And then, right before the fight, Ali told me he had a plan. He was gonna go out and hit Foreman with a straight right hand as soon as the bell rang. I said, 'No champ; no! You're gonna dance.' And he told me, 'No, I'm going out and hit Foreman upside his head, so he'll know he's in a fight.' And that's just what Ali did, but that wasn't the only surprise he had for George that night."

Right: **N'Sele, Zaire, September 16, 1974**
Ali (right) sits with his brother Rahman Ali (formerly Rudy) on the steps of his villa at his training camp. Ali is discussing the news that the world championship prize fight will be postponed because of an injury to his opponent George Foreman.

Rope a Dope

Yes, the surprises were just beginning. In the opening round, the African crowd, chanted "Ali, Bomaye!" (Ali, Kill him!) making the stadium vibrate and hum. But Foreman, strong and in his prime, his eyes ice cold, clearly looked undeterred. Ali embarked on a strategy that he didn't share with his trainer Angelo Dundee, or anyone in his entourage. He ran toward Foreman and hit him with a right-handed lead. He threw twelve right-handed leads in the first round.

The right hand lead is considered an insult in boxing, basically saying that your opponent is too slow to dodge the across-the-body punch. It incensed Foreman no end and he started to swing madly at Ali, throwing haymakers like a kid in a school yard. Round after round he pummeled Ali's arms and sides. But instead of "dancing", Ali leaned back against the ropes, absorbing the blows.

This "rope a dope" was so audacious that author George Plimpton, who was at ringside, turned to Norman Mailer and shrieked: "The fix is in!" thinking Ali was throwing the fight. Angelo Dundee later said, "I won't kid you. When he went to the ropes, I felt sick."

There is a mythology that Ali summoned the rope-a-dope strategy from his agile mind at the moment of the fight. Actually, Ali pulled it out from one of his early trainers, a former boxing great who ironically was in Foreman's corner that night in Kinshasa. As Ali later recalled about the Rope a Dope:

(it) was something Archie Moore used to do. Archie was a smart fighter. He fought till he was as old as I am now, and he did it by conserving energy.

As the fight went on, Ali kept talking to Foreman as Big George rained down his blows: "George you disappoint me!" It was a strategy that resulted in Foreman "punching himself out," tiring after seven rounds just as Ali predicted. In the eighth, Ali punched Foreman off the Rope a Dope with a blow so fierce, perspiration sprayed off of Foreman's head like a burst water balloon. Foreman stumbled to the mat in a lazy semi-circle, and Ali had regained the champion's belt.

Once again Ali shook up the world. This time he even made believers out of his own doubting corner. "I thought George would break him in two," Wali Muhammad remembered. "The plan was to dance for six or seven rounds, tire Foreman out, and when he got tired, move in on him. And instead, Ali was standing in once place, taking punches. A couple of times, I asked Angelo, 'What's happening?' Angelo said, 'I don't know.' Then, in the sixth round, I think it was, Foreman started slowing down. Between rounds, I said, 'Champ; he's getting tired.' Ali told me, 'I know; I'll get him in a couple of rounds.' And that's what he did. He knocked him out in the eighth round. Fighting off the ropes was the wrong thing to do, but it was the right thing to do. Ali just had that ability to see things nobody saw."

Next page: **Kinshasa, Zaire, October 10, 1974**
George Foreman leaves himself wide open to an attack from Ali, who winds up for a fierce strike to his face. Ali knocked Foreman out in the eighth round.

The Thrilla in Manila

When Muhammad Ali returned from Zaire in 1974, he was coming back to a changed nation with an evolving perception of the two-time champion. The mass movements for civil rights and social justice were fading. The U.S. intervention in Vietnam was wheezing to a close, and the memory of Richard Nixon, a casualty of the Watergate scandal, was fading. The establishment sought to make peace with the '60s generation, and suddenly Ali was seen not as a hated divisive political force, but as a new symbol of reconciliation.

The sports media began to appreciate what Ali had done for them. "If you can't write about Ali, you can't write," wrote one of them. Following Zaire, many writers swung from seeing him as "Gaseous Cassius" to a figure of almost incalculable import. *Sports Illustrated* made Ali their 1974 Sportsman of the Year and sportswriter emeritus Maury Allen wrote, "It is time to recognize Ali for what he is: the greatest athlete of his time and maybe all time and one of the most important and brave men of all American time. The time has come to end the bitterness and forget the past."

The ultimate embrace occurred when President Gerald Ford invited Ali to the White House. This was a remarkable turn of events. Just a few short years prior, Ali's phone was being tapped on orders of Ford's boss, Richard Nixon. But the acceptance of Ali was becoming, as Ford consciously realized, a way to use pop culture to put the big, bad '60s to rest. As Ford himself said:

W]hen I took office, we as a nation were pretty much torn apart. There were conflicts between families, in colleges and on the streets ... And one of the major challenges my

administration faced was how we could heal the country. And having Muhammad Ali come to the Oval office was part of our overall effort it was part of my overall effort to heal the wounds of racial division, Vietnam, and Watergate.

The last stage of Ali's reconciliation began on February 25, 1975, with the death of Elijah Muhammad, which led to a split in the Nation of Islam between those who followed Elijah's son Wallace and those who followed Louis Farrakhan. Wallace believed that the NOI was not true Islam and wanted to see an end of the Nation's racialist politics. Farrakhan wanted to continue the "true teachings" of Elijah. Ali went with Wallace—who brought the followers of the Nation of Islam closer to mainstream Islam. It was the final step that allowed Ali to be embraced into the bosom of the establishment.

But Ali without politics, without a movement, without a theater of struggle, was revealed at this point in his life to be all salesman with little to sell. This became clear in numerous ways in his third fight against Joe Frazier, the Thrilla in Manila. The Philippines fight, scheduled for October 1, 1975, was bankrolled by Philippines dictator Ferdinand Marcos. Marcos was in the same league as Mobutu, a corrupt pro-western autocrat, but unlike the Rumble in the Jungle there were no pretensions of Black Power or pride: just a serious money grab in a country gripped by poverty.

In selling the Manila fight, Ali crossed the line from showmanship to a nastiness that tarnished his legacy. He could have riffed that his fight was a battle of political representation, a fight for the winos and dopeheads, against the bigots and Klansmen, but he chose a very different tack.

... I've changed what I believe. What I believe now is true Islam.

Left: **Chicago, February 26, 1975**

Ali addresses a meeting of the Nation of Islam on Muslim Savior Day. To the immediate left of the rostrum is Wallace Muhammad, newly chosen Spiritual Leader and Administrator of the Nation of Islam. Wallace replaced his late father, Elijah Muhammad, whose picture dominates the scene. Breaking with his father's teaching would prove difficult, but Wallace's faith eventually led him to guide the Nation away from a separatist, race-based theology and toward the world community of Islam.

You gotta have a butterfly net to catch me … It's gonna be a chilla, and a killa, and a thrilla, when I get the Gorilla in Manila.

Right: **New York, July 17, 1975**

Ali at a news conference where it was announced he would fight Joe Frazier in Manila on October 1st. He entertained the reporters with some of the more unpleasant aspects of Ali gamemanship by comparing Frazier to a gorilla (he had a toy gorilla in his pocket) and waving a butterfly net.

Crossing the line

In front of his adoring press, Ali took a small rubber gorilla and beat it on the end of a string. As Reggie Jackson said, "This was the one time I was NOT charmed by Ali." Joe Frazier was seen as past his prime, after being demolished by Foreman, but Ali had more than a few distractions of his own. His entourage had swelled to over 50 people. One member of this dicey crew was Ali's mistress Veronica Porche. Her presence would cause a drama that would take Ali's mind off of Joe Frazier, with near fatal results.

For years Ali was somewhat of a tomcat, a "pelvic missionary" as one member of his entourage put it. He himself said, "I used to chase women all the time. And I won't say it was right. But I was young, handsome, and heavyweight champion of the world." For years Ali's wife Khalilah (Belinda) had adopted a "don't ask, don't tell" approach to Ali's extra-marital liaisons.

But with Porche, Ali crossed a line. The problems began when Ali brought her to a press conference, hosted by Ferdinand and Imelda Marcos. When Marcos said to Ali, "You have a beautiful wife," Ali stunned the room by just thanking him, and no one dared correct the dictator. Up to then the media had covered up Porche's presence in Manila but this was too public to ignore. Pete Bonaventre wrote in *Newsweek* :

Solemn Muslim guards have given way to streetwise black, anti-war attitudes have been replaced by wry connoisseurs of his pure showmanship. Even Ali's women, invariably beautiful and black, have now been brought out of the back rooms of his life and openly flaunted. As of last week, Belinda was still at home in Chicago and the stunning Veronica Porche, sometimes known as 'Ali's other wife' was touring Manila with the champ.

Ali, who throughout his career had operated with a sixth sense about how to control the media, made a bad situation worse by holding a press conference to defend his infidelity. He spoke about the "needs of a man" and the desires of a champion. Now Ali was making it a national story and Khalilah, humiliated on an international stage, could no longer stay silent. She boarded a plane for Manila with "a Sonny Liston look in her eye" and went straight to Ali's hotel.

The six-foot Khalilah started "hurling whatever she could get her hands on." Then in a manner as regal as her steely-eyed arrival, she emerged from the hotel, stepped into her limo, and left for home. Khalilah had made quite a stir. As documentarian Leon Gast said, "More people were talking about Veronica-Belinda than Ali-Frazier."

As Ali juggled his personal soap opera, Frazier's fury at Ali's gamesmanship was building into something ugly, even deadly. "It's real hatred," he said. "I want to hurt him. I want to take his heart out." Mark Kram in *Sports Illustrated* wrote of Frazier:

He was there not seeking victory alone; he wanted to take Ali's heart out and then crush it slowly in his hands. One thought of the moment days before, when Ali and Frazier with their handlers between them were walking out of the Malacañang Palace, and Frazier said to Ali, leaning over and measuring each word, "I'm gonna whup your half-breed ass.

A terrible toll

When the fight began, it was 10:45 A.M. and more than 110 degrees, with ungodly humidity. The conditions were set for a battle between two fighters who wouldn't emerge from the ring as whole as when they arrived. As Jerry Izenberg said, "They weren't fighting for the championship of the world. They were fighting for the championship of each other."

Ali didn't dance in this fight or rope-a-dope. He thought Frazier was over the hill and ripe to be picked. He went out there and just started teasing Frazier with straight lefts and rights. Frazier took those shots, but kept inching, closer and closer, inside Ali's grand reach. By the middle rounds, he started to tee off on the tiring Ali and looked to make good on his promise to take out Ali's heart.

As Kram wrote, "Whatever else might one day be said about Muhammad Ali, it should never be said that he is without courage, that he cannot take a punch. He took those shots by Frazier, and then came out for the seventh, saying to him, 'Old Joe Frazier, why I thought you were washed up.' Joe replied, 'Somebody told you all wrong, pretty boy.'"

But then at the start of the 13th Ali, out of shape, slowed by humidity and Frazier's ungodly punishment, found another gear. The man who as a teenager went "dancin' with Johannson" stood flat-footed and attempted to punch through his opponent's face. Frazier's eyes swelled over, the lids puffing out into a violent blindness. Ali hit his blinded opponent so hard in the jaw that Frazier's scarlet mouthpiece flew into the press row. When the bell rang for the 14th round, Ali walked to the center of the ring and hit Frazier, now completely blind, with nine straight right hands. When Smokin' Joe returned to his corner, the referee had to lead him part of the way like a seeing eye dog. Frazier's manager Eddie Futch had seen enough, and told his gallant, battered protégé that he was stopping the fight. Frazier begged Futch to let him continue but Futch just said, "You couldn't see in the last two rounds. What makes ya think ya gonna see in the 15th? Sit down, son. It's all over. No one will ever forget what you did here today."

Ali rejoiced upon hearing Frazier had thrown in the towel and then collapsed on his stool like he was hit by a sniper's bullet. Ali later said that if Frazier had answered the bell, it might have been him to quit on his stool. He said that feeling "… was like death. Closest thing to dyin' that I know of."

Later when addressing the press he said: "I'm tired of bein' the whole game. Let other guys do the fightin'. You might never see Ali in the ring again." In his suite the next morning he said:

I heard somethin' once. When somebody asked a marathon runner what goes through his mind in the last mile or two, he said that you ask yourself why am I doin' this. You get so tired. It takes so much out of you mentally. It changes you. It makes you go a little insane. I was thinkin' that at the end. Why am I doin' this? What am I doin' here in against this beast of a man? It's so painful. I must be crazy. I always bring out the best in the men I fight, but Joe Frazier, I'll tell the world right now, brings out the best in me. I'm gonna tell ya, that's one helluva man, and God bless him.

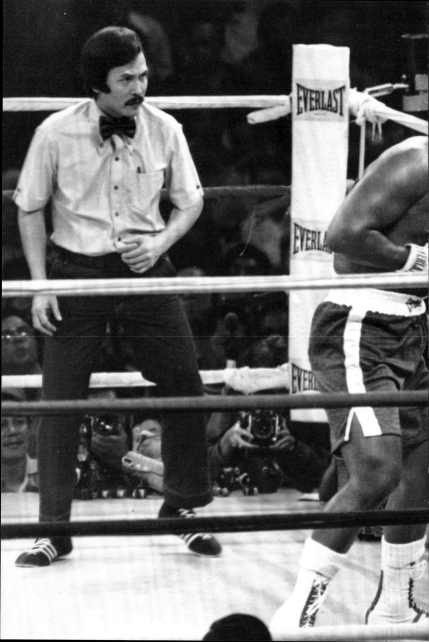

Man, I hit him with punches that'd bring down the walls of a city, Lawdy, lawdy, he's a great champion.

Joe Frazier

Left: **The Coliseum, Manila, Philippines, October 1, 1975**
Ali peeks through his raised gloves as Joe Frazier backs the champion against the ropes in the third round of their title bout, known as "The Thrilla in Manila." Frazier threw in the towel in the fourteenth round.

Interview with Robert Lipsyte

MARYLAND 2006

Robert Lipsyte is an award-winning newspaper and television journalist. His career as a sports journalist began in 1957 when he took what he thought would be a summer job as a copyboy in the sports department of the *New York Times*, a summer job that lasted 14 years. He would return to the *Times* twenty years later. As a newspaper journalist, he wrote sports and city columns for the *Times*, winning Columbia University's Mike Berger Award for distinguished reporting in 1966 and 1996. He was runner-up for the Pulitzer Prize in commentary in 1992. Lipsyte is perhaps best known as a sportswriter for his early coverage of Muhammad Ali. He was one of the few to penetrate Ali's circle, and to recognize the historical importance of the young fighter.

How were you able to connect with the young Cassius Clay /Muhammad Ali, when so many writers looked at him with hostility, as if he was from another planet?

For a lightweight who had grown up in a white ghetto, I was at a point where I had demystified Black people in the sense that I was comfortable liking and hating Black people individually rather than as a group, so I was totally open to Ali and to all the people around him. Also, because I was young, I was not lamed by either the Jackie Robinson or the Joe Louis syndrome, which a lot of the oldest sportswriters were, that the Black athlete was either "a great pioneer" or he was "a credit to his race." I approached Muhammad Ali in the most high-minded and idealistic way, which was "Here is a guy who can advance my career with really good stories." That's how I thought about him. I guess it's pretty healthy.

It's honest. Can you describe that first moment when you saw young Clay; when you were a very young writer he was a very young boxer.

The first time I saw him was a few days before he won the championship. He was 22 and I was a year or two older. Because he's so perfectly proportioned, he seems smaller in pictures and magazines and papers. So the first moment that I actually saw him I was astounded; not only by his beauty but by his enormous size. In one of the great name-dropping moments in history, I have to tell you that the first moment that I saw him, I was standing with the Beatles. The Beatles had been suckered into a photo op at Muhammad Ali's gym because Liston didn't want to be photographed with "those little faggots" as he said, and so the press agent had brought the Beatles down to Ali's gym in a very run-down section of Miami Beach. So the Beatles show up at the gym, the Fifth Street gym, and Ali—Cassius Clay—is not there. They try to leave, but this Wackenhut rent-a-cop service shoved them into a locker room to keep them there for the photo op, and I went in with them. And some time later, when Ali threw open the door and called out, "Hello, Beatles! We're gonna go on the road and make some money"—we all kind of gasped at how big he was.

What about Ali's talking prowess at this first audience? You probably knew before you went to Miami that he was known for having a gift of the gab. Was he like any other athlete you'd covered at that point?

No. He was more like a Bohemian poet than an athlete. We were still operating under the Joe Louis dictum: "I do my talking in the ring." Also I think there was some sense that the braggadocio, the arrogance, was somehow untrue to the Anglo ideal of the athlete, the Anglo "Old West" idea of the laconic gunslinger and hero.

Gary Cooper doesn't say how pretty he is.

Right. What we also didn't understand was that he was coming out of a kind of "Mack" sensibility, a pimp sensibility that says, "I'm so pretty. Hey, c'mon over here, don't you wanna play with me?" and this was something new in sports, something we'd never seen before. Maybe we would have seen it if we had covered ghetto basketball, or sports in the inner cities or in the rural Black neighborhoods— where there's lots more of that intimidation, the dozens, the kind of trash talk back and forth. But we'd never seen this before, and he was the first athlete to break through and bring it with him.

Did the writers of the established Black press at the time have a sense that he wasn't inventing this stuff out of whole cloth—that it was actually coming out of this "Mack" sensibility?

I think they had a sense of that, but they weren't giving it away. I think also that there was some discomfort on the part of bourgeois, middle class Blacks. People don't remember now that, besides the stereotypical conservative hawk reaction to Ali, there was also a real middle-class Black reaction against Ali. He was not in the mold of

Jackie Robinson, Joe Louis, and the first wave of Black ball players in the major leagues. Remember, by this time—we're talking 1964, when he really broke—by this time there was a wave of fine Black ball players who were careful and measured, and kept their mouths shut, and were the ideal of what a Black athlete role model was.

You've written that, when you were covering Miami Beach, Malcolm X's presence was there whether he was in the room or not. What were your impressions of Malcolm at this time?

I liked him, much better than I liked Ali early on. The first time I ever met Malcolm X, his people were "beating me up" at a demonstration out in Brooklyn, and I captured his attention when he said that I had asked a stupid question, and I said "The only stupid question is the one you don't ask"—something I remembered from my sergeant in the Army.

I got to know him much better later on, actually, after he had left the Nation, through Dick Gregory. We spent some time together, and I found him, besides being enormously smart, enormously funny, just a terrific guy. And I think there was a real sadness about his break with Ali.

I think Malcolm had real affection for him. And I think that he knew—he kind of had a sense of what was going to happen to Ali, that he would kind of drift away, ultimately, from the Nation, that it wouldn't work out; and just how—this is hard to say—just how ultimately dumb and exploitable Cassius Clay, Muhammad Ali, has always been.

I think that he has the emotional level of an adolescent at best. I think that his adult interactions are not at a very high level. I think there's an enormous sweetness to him. I think that the current right-wing backlash against him, in the books by Mark Kram, and Suckerpunch, really has less to do with Ali that it has to do with the idea, "He's the liberal hero, so we're going to bring him down as a way of kicking liberal ass," which is ridiculous.

What were your impressions at the time, when you as an individual heard that he had joined the Nation of Islam? Some writers responded as if he'd worn an American flag thong or something.

In retrospect, I have a lot of thoughts, but back then, I thought, "Oh, boy! That's a better story." I found it enormously interesting. I was interested in Malcolm, who I thought was a very interesting guy. I was interested in the Nation of Islam, which seemed to be a voodoo cult religion, but it probably—like a lot of voodoo cult religions, like Hasidim, or those fundamental Christian cults—does clean up some people's lives. The fact is that a lot of the Fruit of Islam were ex-cons, former drug addicts, really leading very responsible lives now because of the Nation of Islam. That's hard to argue against. I didn't really see them as this great, terrible evil that was going to overturn America. I saw them as hypocritical in the sense that they were making connections with segregationists, and what they were saying was certainly against everything I believed in as an integrationist. And I thought [it logical] that Ali had been suckered into a religion. Why wouldn't a kid who'd been brought up the way he was brought up, by this frustrated, spooky father, a Marcus Garvey fan, and a seeker in his own way?

When he became part of this religion he became part of something in which he started to feel better about himself, and once—as they had told him—the white world found out about it, the white world freaked. So now it was like the first time people were afraid of him. Isn't that great for a fighter? So it sounded like a great story; it was great, and he and I really worked well as reporter/subject. But I'm never going to say we were friends; how can you be with your main subject? I spent time with Elijah in his mansion; not really fully understanding all these pregnant teenage secretaries walking barefoot.... The point was that I loved the story. I can't make it more clear that I was, and probably still am, a hired gun. A wordslinger, as I think of myself. I loved the idea that it was a story. Were there people that I thought were better? Yeah, probably. George Foreman, Ernie Terrell, and Floyd Patterson: really good, thoughtful, seeking people. But nowhere near as interesting.

How do you explain these contradictions? You say at one moment that he was "dumb and exploitable," but you also speak about never covering anyone more interesting. On the one hand, he's viewed as someone with a low level of intelligence, on the other hand people talk about how there was never a more intelligent, savvy fighter both in and out of the ring.

Well, Jung said you never grow up until you're able to hold two conflicting thoughts at the same time. Yes, he was dumb and exploitable. But "dumb"—I don't mean not intelligent, just ignorant. I think there was great intelligence of some kind there. Certainly—whatever emotional intelligence is, which I don't understand, but that's probably what it is—he could read people, he was kind of quick, he could understand things. All the low IQs, the bad tests: that's a failure of his schooling, not a failure of his brain. That's what that was about. But it took him a while—to his credit, he got there—before he finally began to figure things out.

But how do we understand the fact that he spoke to something that had not yet fully emerged in his anger about the broken promises of the 1950s, and was a trailblazer by resisting the draft in Vietnam, a war still popular?

I think what we have to make clear is that—and this is hard—in the beginning, at least, he was saying the right things for the wrong reasons, which ultimately doesn't matter because they resonated and they evoked response.

But his reaction against being drafted was a reaction against being drafted, not against war itself. It was "Why draft me when there are poor boys in Louisville? I pay all these taxes, I buy all these guns." He was furious at being reclassified 1A because of the embarrassment of having been classified 1Y for low IQ in the first place. He didn't qualify.

Then they readjusted as they needed more troops. And his attitudes on so many things came out of some sort of sensibility that had not anything to do with the ideological trends of the 60s. Now, what happened is, once he broke from the Muslims, after his title was stripped, after he spent these years in exile going to college campuses, he changed.

Did you go to any of the campus lectures?

Yeah. Eventually, he came to understand who his audience was. And he came to find out where Vietnam was, what Vietnam was about, and then the ultimate idea that white people were sending Black people to kill brown people. I think by the time that he came out of exile in 1970, the things that he was saying made sense to him. That's his quickness; that's his ability to absorb. That's what separated him. I mean, he was a jock. He started boxing when he was twelve years old. It was the total focus of his life. His high school diploma was a gift because they didn't want to stand in the way. So they didn't want to bother him with all the niceties of education like learning how to read. So here is this typical jock, twelve years old, totally focused on one thing. Didn't have to take out the garbage, he just had to box. Totally absorbed in his own career. Illiterate. Ignorant. Then he comes back from the Olympics, and he's bought by the plantation owners of Louisville.

Then he's really a hired piece of meat. He doesn't have to do anything but box. All of a sudden now he's in the warm, and he loves the fame, he loves the joy of it. He's a seeker, though. Something's missing in his life. He can't kiss it off every Sunday in a Baptist meeting. He wants something larger, but he's still an ignorant kid, not the Muhammad Ali of our dreams.

But how does that explain, all these instances where he has the opportunity to waver but he doesn't?
It was his support network, all the people who by this time are looking to him. He's a hero in his own mind as well. He's beginning to understand who he is by people telling him who he is. What would he be giving up? He would be giving up everybody who really believes in him, for what? And he's surrounded day after day after day talking to these Muslims, some of whom are very sophisticated guys who've been places, explaining to him what happens to the Black in America. Ali had enormous support. He was a religionist by this time. He was part of this very powerful religion that was giving him an enormous amount of intellectual and social support. What was his choice? I don't think he had such a choice.

There was this moment in early 1969 when he was shunned by The Messenger when they published the tract saying, "We disavow Muhammad Ali." Can you describe that, what his reaction to that was?

I don't think he really understood what was going on, other than the fact that I think he was beginning to disengage. In May, when—first of all, he was no longer the champion, he was in exile; but he wasn't getting much out of the religion any more. It was the beginning of his awakening. I think maybe he had come to realize he had made a big mistake in being complicitous in Malcolm's death by disavowing him, by stepping aside.

Did he ever speak with you about that?

Yeah, he said he was afraid that he would be killed. I don't know. I think it must be a real sore spot. I was never satisfied with what he had to say. It must have been a tough thing for him. But by now, he was getting this enormous feedback that he had never had before. As he said, he was "the onliest boxer that anyone talked to like a Senator." People would talk to him in this very serious way, taking him seriously. And he was getting off on that too.

And here was a generation, I think that some had honest ideological feelings about the Vietnam war, but a lot of people didn't want to get their brains shot out. That could be considered cowardly. In their own minds, they were afraid to go into the Army. They were afraid to be sent to Vietnam. And here was the heavyweight champion of the world who hung a pair of balls back on them.

You covered Ali when he came back, in 1970–71. How different was the crowd, the atmosphere, around, say, an Ali fight in 1964 compared to 1970?

It was an ocean of difference. The first big fightback he picked, the important fightback, was against Jerry Quarry, in 1970. Everything was different. It was in Atlanta, the new South. It had been arranged by a Black state senator. Lester Maddox, the segregationist governor, did not get in the way. It was an event I'd never seen before. First of all, I'd never seen so many Black people at a boxing match, especially in the good seats. And it was evenly divided between the elite—Abernathy, Mrs. King, Belafonte, the Supremes on one side— and on the other an endless connection of pimps and their hoes in the most amazing finery I'd ever seen. It was a great celebration.

What were they actually celebrating?

The true victory of Black Power. Ali had been in exile for three and a half years. All that meant was that every single boxing commissioner—city, state, all around America, and his passport had been pulled so he couldn't fight overseas—refused to sanction a fight. The title had been stripped already. Nobody would let him fight in America, except the city of the new South, the City That's Too Busy to Hate, aided by a Black state senator, Leroy Johnson. He made it happen. And obviously he could not have made it happen unilaterally. You had to have been complicit in the white power structure in Atlanta. Maybe Ted Turner was involved, who knows? But certainly Maddox laid off. So what could this be but true Black Power? And the return of the Dark Prince in exile? It was an enormously symbolic event.

This is all about the country turning against the war in Vietnam.

The country turned against the war in Vietnam and turned toward Black political power. And also a sense of incredible hope which has not been fully realized by any means. But there was really a sense that something really important was happening in America. And this, in a sense, symbolized it. Ali became a symbol of it. I think it was really less about Ali than the fact that he was there, and he symbolized a moment that captured our dreams and hopes. The big fight with Frazier in the Garden in 1971 was a great spectacle, and it was very exciting, and it was the fight that everyone wanted to see, but in a sense it was back to inside the Beltway. It was a sporting event; I think the Quarry fight was a very cultural event.

Was the sporting event—the Ali-Frazier one—less integrated, as you remember?

Less integrated than the Atlanta fight, but more integrated than previous Garden fights. Now for the rest of the time there would be a much greater Black presence.

Ali made great efforts to paint Frazier as being the "Tom" fighter, the white man's fighter, he said "All the Klansmen will rejoice if Frazier wins," lines like that. Two questions for you: What did you think about that at the time, and the second thing is, did that resonate with people? Did it work?

My reaction was then, and still is now, "How fucking insensitive can you be?" I never thought—and years later, we spoke about it—I never thought that Ali thought that Frazier was a gorilla or a Tom; in any other era Frazier would have been a great heavyweight, a terrific fighter. Ali was selling. In some ways this is harder to take than if he felt it.

It was an ugly sell.

It was an ugly sell, he was selling. So years later Ali would ask "So why'd he take it so badly? I was just trying to hype the fight. He made a lot of money. What's his problem?" But it was an ugly, insensitive sell. I think that in his mind, he saw no great difference between calling Joe a gorilla or an Uncle Tom, a white man's nigger, and calling George Foreman "The Mummy", or Quarry "The Washerwoman", or Floyd Patterson "The Rabbit"; he was just "What's the big deal? Don't be mad at me. I'm just trying to sell our fight, Joe." And Joe was very hurt, I think even more hurt when Ali tried to make people think that he had won that first fight. But I think Ali would do anything. If we find it in our hearts to look upon him as a magical child, as a kind of holy fool, I think it would be easier to understand and appreciate him.

What if Ali wasn't a wise fool? Maybe he could be both. What if he was just a ruthless salesman, and he had a sense about how angry the country was at that time, about who his audience was, and knew that this was the best way to reach his constituency? Is that possible?

I guess so. I would have to re-evaluate my life, and I'll be fucked if I'm going to do that. I don't think so. I don't think so, because I spent so much time with him, and been privy to so many casual acts of compassion and kindness, decency, and wanting to please in small or large ways, that I find it hard to believe that he's some sort of manic real estate salesman going in for the kill. I don't really see that as possible. I don't think that he's that smart. That requires a different kind of cunning and intelligence which I don't think was him. There always was—in talking with high school classmates, they remark about it and I think it's true now—this kind of sweetness that emanates from him which I don't think you can quite fake. Even now, when he can't communicate, he communicates in a kind of— unless I'm being more romantic than you—he communicates in a kind of glow. I don't think he's trying to fake things like that. People would flash on that right away.

Ali said that he wanted to retire when he was 28, "pretty, unmarked, the best of all time." Why did he keep fighting, and fighting and fighting? When did that plan go off the rails? Just like with every athlete, you gotta pull the gloves off?

I think it's really hard to—somebody was once explaining why this aging anchor—he had all the money he needed, why didn't he just quit? And he said, "It's so hard to step out of the warm, the lights of the TV camera." It's always kind of stuck with me. I mean, who's to say? Where would he ever feel again that kind of adulation, attention, where would he feel so alive as in the ring?

The [Earnie] Shavers fight was really the last fight. He joked about it later that he got hit so hard, his ancestors in Africa turned over in their graves. But, I mean, he won that fight, and then afterward, the [Larry] Holmes thing was terrible. [Trevor] Berbick was a tragedy.

How was he a different fighter from the time before his suspension to when he came back? Was he a different fighter?
Yeah, he wasn't as fast, but I think that because he wasn't a fighter—he was really more of a boxer—and because his speed, as wonderful as it was, wasn't the only thing, I think that he was an artist in the ring in the same way [John] McEnroe was an artist, I guess Michael Jordan was an artist, wouldn't you say?

These guys were so creative, and so delicate, and so thinking, and Ali was that. Look at the "rope-a-dope" he unveiled in the Rumble in the Jungle against Foreman. He didn't sit and plan that with his handlers. It came to him. Early on in that fight there's a punch…where Foreman really hits him really hard in the neck. And you see him thinking, "Holy shit, this guy can hurt me!" And so he retreated to the ropes, to think about this—what he was going to do—George lumbers after him, and starts hitting him. And suddenly Ali is saying, "He's hitting me on my arms! And they're gonna go dead before my arms go dead." And so he created this brilliant scheme. You can see that in other fights, where he choreographs things, where things come to him.

Didn't Dundee say he had very little control over plans?
What would Dundee say? "Circle around, stay away from his left"— what trainers always say. "Cut the ring on him. Don't let him hit

you." He also had to be creative and artistic because, unlike Frazier, he was unwilling to get hit in order to hit back. So in many ways, if you look at some of the fights like [Foley], Williams, where he choreographs something in his mind, maybe at the last minute, whatever it is—Alvin Ailey is out there boxing. After he comes back, I don't think he's quite as able to do that, simply because he can't rely on his speed to get him out of danger any more. So he is punching a little more, he's absorbing a little more, but he's also more creative and more daring.

The raw statistics of the number of punches that he takes after he comes back compared to before is shocking. The Cleveland Lance fight, he took eight punches the whole fight, and Frazier was in the triple digits. How did you feel, watching the fight in Manila?

No. It was the fight in New York against Frazier that I decided I was leaving sportswriting. I think that probably, despite what seems like my harsh analyses and all, I was very emotionally involved with him. I liked him. I still like him, I like him a lot. But more than that, I do understand he made my career. And at that fight, I was at ringside with a telephone, reporting back to the desk because they wanted a replay, go back with another edition as soon as the fight was over, but I was not writing at ringside.

So I was giving them what was happening, and after a round or two I started giving a blow-by-blow, my first and only play-by-play, and they patched me in all over the *Times*. In hearing a tape of it later, I realized that anybody who was listening to my play-by-play would have been convinced that Ali was winning the fight big. That's how I was seen. I came to realize that I just got too emotionally involved.

Did his loss against Frazier affect you personally, seeing him go down to that big left hook?

I was very disappointed. I felt very bad for him. This is not how I wanted to live my life. I did not want to get involved with my subjects—the athletes—in those ways. And I realized he was the most interesting thing for me in sports; I was not that much interested in other things. I had been at the *Times* for fourteen years; the column was four years, and I had done everything I wanted to do at that point. I'd grown up wanting to write fiction, so I wanted to go back writing fiction full time.

I wanted to ask you what you thought when you saw Ali light the Olympic torch in 1996.

I had chills. It was amazing, with shaky hand, I thought about—he was so right. He was absolutely the right person to do that. In Atlanta—that connection, he had been an Olympic gold medal winner, I just thought it was great and also maybe the most famous patient in America. It was his Parkinson's. Who else has been out there in that way, in terms of what he's done for so many sick or disabled people. To be able to go out there so unselfconsciously—that's got to be one of, in many ways—that has to be even a more powerful statement of empowerment to sick and isolated hurt people than being against the war was for college boys who were afraid of getting sent to Vietnam. So I thought it was a great act of—could have been narcissism, but I thought it was courage. I thought it was wonderful; I thought it was great.

A couple months ago I wrote about Ali receiving the Presidential Medal of Freedom from Bush, and Bush calling him a "great man of peace." The thing these two guys had in common was that they both got out of Vietnam, one very publicly, the other… different. What are your thoughts on that?

I think it was disgusting, myself. It's something you gotta deal with. It doesn't compute in a way in which you want to believe in Muhammad Ali and what you thought Muhammad Ali stood for.

How could he accept this? I'm not even asking Muhammad Ali to make a statement, just quietly tell whoever called, "Mr. Ali can't accept the medal." Just keep it quiet. This is back to your Jungian problem of holding conflicting thoughts.

Do you see Ali as basically a prisoner of events, led around by Lonnie, or do you think he has some personal agency?

Of course he has personal agency. The personal agency is "I'm going to the White House, and the President's going to hang a medal around my neck, and I'm going to be on television." Now maybe he can take it to some higher level and say, "I'm going to inspire all these little Black kids, and it's going to be good for my museum in Louisville, and Parkinson's patients are going to feel better about themselves," I don't know. I would like to think that he had those kind of thoughts, but I think basically he's champion again. He's back in the warm. And that's gotta be OK. That really has to be OK.

I think that we have to realize that it's the Muhammad Ali of our minds. That's the one that exists. Muhammad Ali is kind of a hologram in our minds. I think that we've created him, and he exists. Different Muhammad Alis for different people. And I've found that the Muhammad Ali who lit the Olympic torch was inspiring and a hero and gave me chills, and the Muhammad Ali who accepted the medal from George Bush was a narcissistic fool who disgusted me. And they're the same guy, and I like him.

chapter 6

We all grow old

A fading star: 1978–the present

There is an old boxing expression that there is no such thing as a fighter who leaves the sport "on time." No one walks away. Everyone limps. The young Cassius Clay was determined to break that trend and go off into the sunset "thirty years old, rich, pretty, the best of all time." Even his detractors believed he had a chance to leave on his own terms since the young Clay was simply too quick to be touched. Of course no one could have foreseen a three-year ban, escalating debt, and an addiction to the fame of being champion: what journalist Robert Lipsyte calls "the warm." And even his most ardent supporters could never have foreseen that this "butterfly" would have a chin like a piece of granite. Ali's tremendous, almost otherworldly, capacity to endure punishment, and his inability to leave the spotlight, defined the rest of his career. But inside that skull of rock was a brain that had endured hell in Manila and would never be quite right again.

After Manila, his handlers were determined to cash in. Ali was a willing participant in a schedule that included books, movies, television, comics, and five fights in under two years.

Previous page: **Olympic Stadium, Atlanta, July 19, 1996**
Ali uses the Olympic torch to ignite the Olympic flame as the American swimmer Janet Evans looks on during the opening ceremony.
Right: **Los Angeles, July3, 1979**
Muhammad Ali with his wife, Veronica Porche, and his mother, Odessa Grady Clay, for the announcement of an entertainment extravaganza to be held in his honor on September 6, 1979.

Money, money, money!

The motivation wasn't merely that he loved "the warm" but because he needed the money. As Dave Kindred wrote:

Despite fifteen years in the ring and 40 million dollars, Ali lived from paycheck to paycheck. It all went somewhere. Taxes, the Nation, Herbert's one third cut, Dundee's fees, salaries for his entourage, handouts to assorted hangers-on, divorce settlements, agreements with women claiming to be mothers of illegitimate children. (Dundee once pointed to an electrical socket and said, 'If he stuck his dick in there, that light socket would get pregnant.')

In February 1976 Ali fought a Belgian boxer named Jean-Pierre Coopman, nicknamed for the fight by Ali's promotion team, "The Lion of Flanders." Coopman was a fifth rate fighter. The bout was designed to let fans bask in Ali the showman and it ended mercifully in Ali winning a fifth-round knock out.

Then, in April 1976, he took on journeyman Jimmy Young in what was supposed to be another cakewalk. This fight became archetypal of the rest of Ali's career. It went the full 15 rounds and although he won a unanimous decision, the bout was far more draining that it should have been. Ali was a soft 230 pounds, and like any "athlete in winter," his body wasn't doing what his mind was telling it. Any boxer who hangs on too long flirts with catastrophe. A short 24 days later on May 24, 1976, Ali fought again against Richard Dunn. The fight was in Munich and nowhere close to a sellout. Ali bought and gave away 2,000 tickets to members of the U.S. armed forces stationed in West Germany. A kind gesture, without question, but Ali's comments further reflected the absence of a political rudder. "If I was a soldier, I would want to see me; and I got nothing against them for going into the army. I didn't go because of my religion but them soldiers are just doing their job."

This absence of a political stand was also seen in revelations that his promotional team was attempting to negotiate a big pay-day for Ali to fight in apartheid South Africa. The racist regime of South Africa looked to Ali for the same reason Mobutu and Marcos wanted the Champ: legitimacy and an easy PR win.

The deal fell through, but for reasons financial, not political. It was not that Ali didn't care about the plight of oppressed blacks in South Africa—it's that he was largely unaware of it. His manager, Herbert Muhammad, attempted to justify the flirtation with Nation of Islam rhetoric, but the episode was a sad political echo of the past.

On June 25, 1976, Ali finally crossed over to professional wrestling, in an exhibition match against "sports entertainment" pioneer Antonio Inoki. It was a fifteen-round disaster, with Inoki apparently becoming nervous about being punched, departing from the script and crab walking around the ring, kicking at Ali's legs. Ali was able to throw only six punches the whole fight, and "won" a decision. Afterward he was sheepish, saying "I didn't know he was going to fight like that."

The humiliation was made worse when Ali had to be hospitalized for blood clots in his legs as a result of Inoki's low, awkward kicks. As an increasingly disillusioned Dr. Ferdie Pacheco said years later, "To subject a great, legendary fighter to a carnival atmosphere was wrong."

Bread and circuses

All of Ali's fights were now carnivals. His next bout on September 28, 1976 was a six million dollar payday against the jawbreaker himself, Ken Norton. Ali worked hard to get himself in shape for the Madison Square Garden bout, but if the fight itself was all business, outside the ring it was chaos. The police were on strike and street criminals crashed the gate to rub shoulders with boxing's higher class brigands in the front row.

The fight was rough for Ali, who was now almost 35 years old. Norton dominated the early rounds and seemed to be coasting to victory. But Ali's stubborn will, which transcended the carnival atmosphere, would not let him quit or go down. He stormed back and the fight was even going into the 15th round.

As referee Arthur Mercante described it, he overheard Angelo Dundee telling Ali to stay aggressive, and Norton's corner telling their valiant fighter to hang back. This was disastrous advice that cost Norton the championship. "I look back and wish I could fight that last round again," Norton said. "I was hurt. I was angry. I was upset. I never watched a tape of that fight."

Left: **Budokan Hall, Tokyo, June 26, 1976**
Ali signed up to fight Japanese wrestler Antonio Inoki for what was billed as the World's Martial Arts Championship. Unable to fight like a boxer, or a wrestler, he resorted to verbal abuse, taunting, wisecracks, and an occasional sticking out of his tongue The 15-round bout ended in a draw.

There is no question now that Ali is through as a fighter. The hard work, the life and death in Manila, the endless parade of women provided by fools close to him, have cut him down ...

Mark Kram

Left: **New York City, September 25, 1976**
Challenger Ken Norton smiles at Ali as they square off in the corridor after taping a segment for CBS TV before their fight at Yankee Stadium on September 28th.

Do you know how tired I am?

It was now crystal clear that Ali was on a frightening downward trajectory. In addition to the erosion of his skills, Ali's divorce from Khalilah was finalized, his marriage to Veronica Porche was being planned, and he had book and movie deals in the works. It was a time of pressure, and pain. Like most controversial great athletes, the place Ali found refuge was in plying his trade. But the fights became endurance tests against boxers that the young Ali would have picked off in the round of his choosing.

On September 29, 1977, Ali was due to fight against the hardest punching heavyweight alive, Earnie Shavers. In the days before the fight Ali and his entourage began to feel misgivings about the pain in store. Long-time sports scribe Jerry Izenberg remembered sitting with Ali before the fight and Ali saying to him:

Do you know how many years I've been fighting? Do you know how tired I am? Do you know how hard that man is going to beat on my head tomorrow night?

Izenberg asked him why he did it, but Ali just mumbled in response, his words already becoming slurred. The "Louisville Lip" had started to lose his voice, and there were still many rounds of boxing to go.

Opposite: **Ali marries Veronica Porche, Los Angeles, June 19, 1977**
The couple pose for photographers, following their wedding. It was the third marriage for Ali.

The Shavers-Spinks fights

The Shavers fight drew 77 million viewers, and an amazing 54.4 rating (over 54% of TV sets in use were watching the fight.) Once again, the fight went 15 rounds. Once again, Ali was terribly hurt, saying later that "only Joe Frazier" had ever hit him harder. Once again he squeaked out a decision. Ironically, Ali being hurt may have saved him in the fight. As Shavers recalled, "In the second round, I hit him with a right hand that hurt him. He wobbled and then he wobbled some more. But Ali was so good at conning, I thought he was playing possum with me. I didn't realize how bad off he was. Later when I watched the tape, I saw it, but at the time I was fooled. He could do that. That's why he was Ali."

After the Shavers fight, people close to Ali tried to move heaven and earth to get him to retire. In the cutthroat mercenary world of boxing, there were remarkable acts of empathy on display. Teddy Brenner, the Madison Square Garden "matchmaker," held a press conference to say, "As long as I'm here, Madison Square Garden will never make Ali an offer to fight again. This is a young man's game. Ali is 35. He has half his life ahead of him. Why take chances? There's nothing more for him to prove. I don't want him to come over to me some day and ask, 'What's your name?'" Quite ironic that the same New York boxing establishment that sparked Ali's unconstitutional ban nine years earlier, was now blacklisting him out of the goodness of their heart.

The following week, Dr. Ferdie Pacheco left as well, saying, "the Shavers fight was the final straw for me." Pacheco claims he had a report that Ali's kidneys were failing. He says he submitted these reports to Herbert Muhammad, Dundee and Ali's wife Veronica. When they didn't even deign to respond, Pacheco knew "it was time to go." Yet as Dave Kindred wrote, "What Pacheco couldn't know but suspected was that Ali's brain bled as well."

Ali's people instead scheduled what they thought would be another cream-puff fight, against 1976 U.S. Olympic gold medalist Leon Spinks. Spinks was just 7-0 when the fight was announced. He was also a notorious drug and alcohol abuser. This looked good to Ali who thought he could bill it as "Ali defeats the Olympian" just like he defeated Olympic gold medalists Patterson, Frazier, and Foreman. Spinks even tore a muscle in his shoulder preceding the bout, but his promoters wouldn't let him bow out, fearing, correctly, that the public appetite for Ali-Spinks was so small—and Spinks was so volatile—he would never get another chance. Spinks was shot up with painkillers, and beat Ali over 15 rounds. Ali tried to rope-a-dope as he had against Foreman, but Spinks never punched himself out and Ali had no power coming off the ropes. Spinks won by split-decision and it wasn't even that close.

For the first time, Ali had lost his title in the ring. Ali's people were screaming that their man was robbed, but Ali was never the kind of athlete to make excuses. *New York Times* Pulitzer Prize winning writer Dave Anderson wrote in the fight's aftermath, "[Ali's] face. That wonderful face which once was hardly ever marked in a fight suddenly seemed stretched and aged as he plodded out for the final round. And now, up close, there were purple bruises above and below his right eye and over the bridge of his nose. His forehead was swollen near his left eye. Blood from his cut lower lip spotted his white satin trunks and his white terry-cloth robe."

That night at 2 A.M. Ali was jogging along the Chicago Freeway muttering, "Gotta get my title back." He wasn't close to being done.

… I messed up. I was lousy. But I don't want to take anything away from Spinks. He fought a good fight and never quit. He made fools of everyone. Even me.

Left: **Las Vegas, Nevada, February 16, 1978**
Ali hooks his left about the neck of Leon Spinks in the World Championship Heavyweight fight. Spinks won the title by a split decision.

Ali-Spinks: the rematch

The public wanted to see Ali rise one last time and he wanted desperately to give it to them. For the rematch, he pushed his body harder than any 36-year-old should.

The fight played out on September 16, 1978 in front of the largest sports audience in TV history and 63,000 people in the New Orleans Superdome. It was a long, drawn-out dirge, in which Ali out-pointed a foggy-eyed Spinks. Ali became boxing's first three-time champion. It seemed like the correct time for Ali to retire after enduring his fifth straight fifteen-round fight in less than two years. He answered the retirement rumors saying:

I'd be the biggest fool in the world to go out a loser after being the first three-time champ. None of the black athletes before me ever got out when they was on top. My people need one black man to come out on top. I've got to be the first.

After nine months Ali announced his retirement with his old vaudeville buddy Howard Cosell. As Dave Kindred wrote:

Never did he look more pitiable with Cosell. His face was puffy, his eyes lost, his voice an airy gurgle. He didn't seem able to smile.

Cosell asked Ali if he was at peace with retirement. Ali answered:

Yes sir, Howard. So glad that it's all over. I'm glad that I'm still intelligent enough to speak. I'm glad that I'm the three-time champion. I'm glad I got to know you. And thank you for all the backing. I remember when the Vietnam crisis was going, you'd go on television and say, 'If you don't believe Muhammad Ali is champion then get in the ring with him.' I want to say you helped me during my exile.

Cosell then asked him, "You're the greatest aren't you?" Ali barely managed a grimace, and the warm glow of the camera could not even coax one of his trademark boasts from him. "I try to be," he said. "Maybe it's just you thinking."

What Ali didn't know then was that there would be two further bouts to endure, both of which have been described not as boxing matches but tragedies—and some said that they were crimes.

All my life, I knew the day would come when I'd have to kill myself. I dreaded it and now it's here. I've never suffered like I'm forcing myself to suffer now ... All the time I'm in pain. I hurt all over, I hate it. But I know this is my last fight, and it's the last time I'll ever have to do it.

Left: **The Superdome, New Orleans, Louisiana, September 16, 1978**
Ali ties up Leon Spinks during their heavyweight title fight rematch, in which he regained the world title for an unprecedented third time in front of 64,000 fans.

Desperate measures

Muhammad Ali in retirement was neither happy nor at peace. He and Veronica lived in a lavish Los Angeles mansion with enough knick-knacks to fill an antebellum museum, but it wasn't enough. Veronica especially was enamored with the finer things and would buy antique chairs with accompanying velvet ropes so guests would know that these were not for sitting on but gazing at. Ali's third wife demanded an expensive lifestyle, but due to years of negligence, thievery, and his own generous, trusting nature, the champ who had earned more than 40 million dollars in the ring, was nearly broke.

As associate, Gene Dibble, remembered:

It didn't take a genius to hustle Ali. In the ring he might have been the smartest man ever, but when it came to money, knowing who to trust, his decisions weren't very smart. I've never seen a man who made so much money… (have) such tremendous disregard for money.

Ali's popularity after the Spinks fight was so high, people came out of the woodwork to cash in on Ali-fever. Yet unlike modern superstars like Michael Jordan or Tiger Woods, Ali showed a tremendous disregard for the value and credibility of his name as a "brand." He signed off his name on a short-lived fast-food chain called "Champburgers," a line of exercise equipment, candy bars, sodas, even an Ali car. Most of these deals were either undercapitalized and folded quickly, or were rip-off scams. The problem would compound itself when a legitimate business would approach Ali about an endorsement or investment deal and he more often than not was already bound by contract to another company.

Then there was the political legacy of Ali, which even though he was long past making political speeches, made him toxic to some sectors of corporate America. As a former business manager of Ali's told Thomas Hauser: "I went to a lot of people at major department stores trying to sell Muhammad Ali sportswear. These were buyers, store presidents, CEOs. And invariably the response I got was, 'Harold, you're crazy! For years we've been trying to keep blacks out of our stores … Why should we carry a product line that invites them in?' … And below the Mason-Dixon Line, forget it … And at that time, which was 1980, let's face it, no black athlete had been successful selling his name."

A return to the ring began to be seen by Ali as the one place where he could secure his financial future. While Ali's financial situation inexorably pulled him back to boxing, so did his inability to find a place for himself, a platform for his personality, outside the ring. This was seen most clearly in 1979 when President Jimmy Carter—for reasons that are still incomprehensible—decided to send Ali to Africa on a diplomatic mission to try to win the African continent to join the U.S. boycott of the 1980 Olympics in Moscow. Ali jumped at the opportunity to be "the black Kissinger." The trip, however, was a disaster, called by *Time* magazine "the most bizarre diplomatic mission in recent U.S. history."

First and foremost, many African leaders saw his visit as an insult, a slap in the face from Carter. One Tanzanian official asked, "Would the United States send Chris Evert to negotiate with London?" It also failed because African leaders were giving Ali a crash course in the strained relations between the United States and the African continent. Ali was forced, as he later put it very aptly, to "take a whuppin for U.S. policies."

A failed political pawn

African leaders rebuffed Ali harshly, asking why should they respect the Olympic boycott after the United States refused to support them in 1976 when 29 African nations boycotted the Montreal Summer Games in opposition to apartheid South Africa. Ali, always honest and never the politician, responded by saying:

Maybe I'm being used to do something that ain't right. You're making me look at things different. If I find out I'm wrong, I'm going back to America and cancel the whole trip.

When a diminished Ali returned to the U.S. the wheels were already turning for a comeback. He needed his platform, he needed the money, but he also needed the attention and the rush. He told a friend, "I don't care how much money you have. I don't care who your friends are. There's nothing like the sound of the crowd when you come down that aisle and they're yelling, 'Ali!' 'Ali!'" Ali was set to fight heavyweight champion Larry Holmes on October 2, 1980. The worries that a 38-year-old, overweight, visibly slowed Ali would be destroyed in the ring were immediately voiced. Even his mother Odessa went to the press to say "I don't want to see him fighting anymore." Ferdie Pacheco also chimed in saying that the fight should not be allowed.

Right: **Concord Baptist Church, New York, October 20, 1980**
Ali applauds a speech by President Jimmy Carter during a campaign stop.

"I want Holmes. Gimme Holmes!"

To quell public anxiety, the Nevada Boxing Commission took the unprecedented step of making Ali go through a battery of tests at the Mayo Clinic in Minnesota before allowing the fight with Holmes to go forward. The Mayo clinic found many red flags including diminished motor skills and slurred speech, but the Commission upon seeing the report determined that the fight would go on.

There could not have been a worse opponent for Ali than Larry Holmes. Not only was Holmes young, tough, and hungry, he had also been Ali's sparring partner for four years until the ripe age of 24. He even went to Zaire to train with Ali before the Foreman fight. Therefore, the only conceivable advantage Ali could have over this younger, stronger, man was his mystique. It was the Ali magic that slowed Earnie Shavers when he was convinced a stumbling Ali was "playing possum." But Holmes had seen Ali behind the curtain and knew his every trick. Holmes' trainer said:

When the time came, Larry didn't want to fight Ali. He knew Ali had nothing left; he knew it would be a horror. But once the offer was on the table, he couldn't turn it down.

Right: **Las Vegas, Nevada, October 2, 1980**
Larry Holmes pounds Ali. Holmes won when Ali failed to answer the bell to start the 11th round.

Sacrificed by his promoters

Once the promotion was under way, it was clear that Holmes, nicknamed the "Easton Assassin," would be a pitiless opponent. Ali joked in the pre-fight press conference that Holmes had a head like a peanut. Holmes simply said:

I'll out-jab him. If he covers up, I'll break his ribs or murder his kidneys ... I'll beat him to death. He's in trouble.

As the fight approached, Ali shed his weight and reporters willingly began to fall under his spell. They predicted victory for the old warrior and the odds began to shift in Ali's favor. Like a high school reunion, it seemed all the reporters wanted one last walk down memory lane, but it was a brutal exercise in self-deception.

They should have known that Ali was painfully overmatched. What they didn't know was that in the lead-up to the fight, Ali had been misdiagnosed as having a thyroid problem. Elijah Muhammad's former personal doctor started prescribing him the thyroid medicine, Thyrolar. This sped his metabolism, which helped him shed the weight, but it left him listless in the fight.

Thyrolar prevents the body from cooling down and can sap a person of their energy when engaged in normal physical exertion. In the context of a heavyweight title fight, the medicine could have been fatal.

Holmes could easily have killed Ali. The fight—memorably described by the actor Sylvester Stallone as "an autopsy on a man who was still alive"—lasted ten rounds, with Holmes winning all ten. At one point, Holmes hit Ali in the kidneys—his failing kidneys—so hard that Ali yelped in pain. For the writers who had been in love with Ali for almost two decades, the entire fight became an atrocity and too difficult to bear. The sports commentator Jerry Izenberg expressed the feelings of many onlookers when he said:

I tried to be professional. But then that round when Holmes unloaded and landed that awful hook to the kidneys, when Ali stood there covering his face with his hands, I died. I felt horrible. I said to myself, 'Please don't let him get hurt.' And I started shouting, "Stop it! Stop the fight!"

Afterward, Holmes visited Ali in his hotel room to say that he loved him. Ali, sitting, smiled and said, "I want Holmes! Gimme Holmes!" Holmes could only smile back, but later there was no celebration. It was an ugly night and Holmes knew it.

The main winner of the fight, even more than Holmes, was promoter Don King. King controlled Holmes and now controlled the heavyweight championship. Writer John Schulian, after cursing Don King's name, said of the promoter and his cohorts:

They sacrificed Ali. That's all it was, a human sacrifice for money and power.

Don King views fighters the way a snake views frogs: like something to eat.

Jeremiah Shabazz

Left: **Sardi's, West 44th St., New York City, January 1, 1981**
Boxing promoter Don King, right, and heavyweight champion Larry Holmes wearing contrasting mink coats. Three months before, Holmes, Ali's former sparring partner, had stopped Ali in the 11th round in Las Vegas, the first time Ali had failed to go the distance.

Endgame: Ali's last fight

The day after the Holmes fiasco columnist Hugh McIlvanney, one of the writers who had talked up a possible Ali win, wrote:

The ring activities of Muhammad Ali now have all the grace and sporting appeal of Russian roulette played with a pump-action shotgun. If he seriously considers inflicting upon himself and his admirers across the world another experience like Thursday night's disaster in Las Vegas, there may be a case for taking him into protective custody.

If the fight against Holmes was an execution that no one wanted to see but everyone had to watch, then Ali's final fight against Trevor Berbick was something people were only too glad to ignore. Here was Ali, perhaps the most important athlete of the 20th century, and not a single network or closed circuit television company deigned to broadcast the bout. The fight was so forgettable that many people today still refer to Ali's last fight as being against Holmes, with Berbick a forgotten figure. Even the fight's promotional name "The Drama in the Bahamas," sounded like a Saturday Night Live parody of Ali's earlier great bouts "The Rumble in the Jungle" or the "Thrilla in Manila."

The only "drama" in the Bahamas occurred when the fight was delayed for two hours because the promoters lost the key to the outdoor arena (actually the front gate of a baseball field) where the fight was supposed to take place. Then the "drama" continued when they couldn't find the ring bell and a cowbell taken from the front seat of someone's truck was used in its place. Ali would come in with a bang, but go out with a cowbell. There was certainly no drama in the fight itself. Ali somehow lasted ten rounds, with Berbick winning nine. Berbick was almost sheepish in the ring, embarrassed that someone of his limited skill could so easily handle the great Ali.

Outside the ring, a far more intriguing, and brutal beat-down took place. Don King, furious at not getting a cut from this very small gate, went down to the islands to confront promoter James Cornelius, an ex-con who was very tight with the Nation of Islam. King ended up in the hospital, a "victim of a savage beating."

While King staggered out of the Bahamas, Ali was able to leave with a touch of grace, saying to reporters, "I didn't show and now I know." Ali's ring career was over, but he was about to face a foe that takes no prisoners and has never been defeated, a foe that beat his brain from the inside-out.

Next page: **Nassau, Bahamas, December 11, 1981**
Ali takes a punch from Canadian Trevor Berbick during the first round of their ten-round bout. For Ali, who lost on a unanimous decision, this was his last fight.

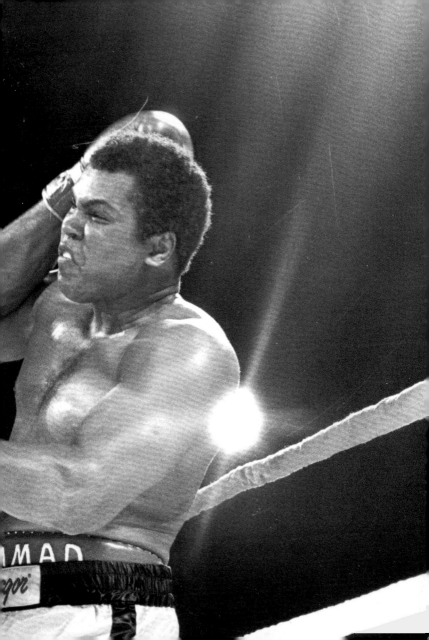

A prisoner in his own body

He was once known as the "Louisville Lip," "Cash the Brash," "Mighty Mouth" and "Gaseous Cassius". He promoted fights by spitting verses at the denizens of Greenwich Village's legendary coffee houses. He starred on Broadway, cut albums, did a whirlwind college speaking tour, and was "the onliest boxer they talk to like a senator." But Muhammad Ali, he of the golden tongue, was entering a prison of silence. The man who had "shook up the world" was speaking in the familiar language of slurred speech, and garbled sounds, the lexicon of every boxer who didn't know when to quit.

By 1984, Ali was the subject of "Saturday Night Live" parodies by stand-up impressionists, his breathy southern voice mocked as though he had a mouth full of marbles. Most believed that Ali was "punch drunk," known medically as chronic encephalopathy. But the pounding Ali took at the end of his career had produced something far worse: Parkinson's disease, a severe illness of the nervous system that affects speech, movement, and even facial expressions. Parkinson's was slowly accomplishing what Joe Frazier, Sonny Liston, and the U.S. Government could not: it was silencing Ali.

One of the insidious effects of Parkinson's is that the thinking process or intelligence of an individual is largely unchanged. Parkinson's is not a lobotomy. But you become a prisoner in your own body, almost entirely unable to communicate what emotions may be building within.

In 1984, Ali was brought to a hospital in new York to undergo a battery of tests. He said to reporters: "I'm not suffering. I'm in no pain. It's really nothing I can't live with. But I go to bed every night … and two hours after I get up, I'm tired and drowsy again. Sometimes I have trembling in my hands. My speech is slurred …

I'm not scared but my family and friends are scared to death."

Doctors subsequently issued a statement to the press that Ali did NOT have Parkinson's but was exhibiting "mild symptoms of Parkinson's syndrome." It was a bizarre diagnosis that posed more questions than it answered. The hospital's statement ended with an assurance that Ali would be able to "carry out personal appearances and other business activities indefinitely." This maddening inconclusiveness meant that for a period of years Ali was approached by all kinds of quacks with highly expensive treatments aimed at reversing his condition. The same way Ali attracted all kinds of social parasites in his fight days, now unsavory elements in the medical community arrived at his door, ready to feast on his largesse, and Ali was desperate to seek a miracle cure. But there was no cure: just dashed hopes and a creeping infirmity.

As Dave Kindred wrote:

Boxing had robbed him of middle age. He was an old man at 41. He couldn't sleep at night and might fall asleep during the day standing up. Walking, he was not sure where his feet would come down next. His face, that pretty face, accomplice to his mischief—now puffy, stiff, more a mask than a face.

Next page: **New York, September 21, 1984**
Ali speaks to reporters about his Parkinson's syndrome diagnosis, with Rev. Jesse Jackson looking on. His neurologist says he could not tell whether the disease was caused by head blows.

Dr. Ferdie Pacheco said, "[In the past] if he was joyful, every muscle showed it. Now, most of the time, he's got that dull flat look. And I hate it. If that's what boxing does, then it shouldn't be a sport. But this is not what boxing does. This is what boxing does if you stay on too long … The three greatest fighters of all time—Joe Louis, Sugar Ray Robinson, and Muhammad Ali—each fought past the age when they should have stopped and they all wound up physically impaired. There's a message in that for anyone who's paying attention."

Ali's condition forced the generation of writers who made their careers filling their notebooks with Ali's exploits, to confront the terrible underbelly of boxing. In 1984, George Plimpton visited Ali at his Los Angeles mansion and was devastated by what he saw:

I saw him sitting at his desk working laboriously to sign his name. He wasn't even a shadow of what I had seen before. And despite being filled with beautiful things, his house seemed so empty, so bare.

The emptiness of Ali's home was generated not only by his medical condition but his failing marriage to Veronica. She had signed on to be the wife of the heavyweight champion of the world, not of a physically damaged man who would require near constant care. They divorced in the summer of 1986, with Veronica walking away with more money than Ali, further damaging his financial security. Veronica also left with their two daughters, Hana and Laila, taking away a network of immediate emotional support he desperately needed.

Ali was being smothered by that common outgrowth of

Parkinson's sufferers: clinical depression. As Ali said in his recent book *The Soul of a Butterfly* (co-written with his daughter Hana Ali):

As a man who spent most of my life developing his physical fitness and athleticism, [Parkinson's] was difficult to accept. At first there were times when I could push all thoughts of the disease out of my mind. Later when the physical symptoms could not be ignored, there were periods of frustration and depression which I had to fight as vigorously as any opponent I faced in the ring.

The public's perception of Ali worsened when Dave Kindred, in a searing series of articles in the *Atlanta Journal-Constitution,* uncovered an elaborate hoax where Ali's lawyer Richard Hirschfeld was calling senators, reporters, and business people, impersonating Ali for his own ends. Hirschfeld had a number of plans for what he could achieve with Ali's voice, but his main goal was to influence the U.S. senate to change the law so that Ali could sue the government for lost wages during his period of exile. As Ali's lawyer, Hirschfeld stood to get a third of what could have been an eight-figure windfall.

Even though Ali had limited knowledge of Hirschfeld's actions, it made him look even more helpless, more infirm. In fact, what tipped Kindred off to wrongdoing was an article in the *Washington Post* that described Ali as politically lucid and incisive. There is no way, Kindred reasoned, that Ali could be making these statements since he was anything but lucid and incisive. In addition to being a colossal embarrassment, the story further increased the perception that Ali desperately didn't want: that he was an object of pity.

Meeting Lonnie

These revelations, compounded with his medical condition, sent Ali further into a hole, where he limited public appearances, and stayed out of the spotlight. "I didn't like the idea of being dependent on medications," he said. "For a while I refused to take my medication consistently. I even went through a period where I wouldn't do television interviews, mainly because I didn't want people feeling sorry for me, and I didn't want to let my fans down. My shaking and soft speech were harder to accept."

But in 1986, something happened that began to reveal a light at the end of the tunnel, and a broader sense of purpose: Muhammad Ali married his fourth wife, Yolanda "Lonnie" Williams. They married in 1986, but Lonnie and Muhammad first met in 1962 when the Williams family moved across the street in Louisville from Odessa and Cassius Clay, Sr., and the two mothers became fast friends. At that time, Lonnie was just five and a half years old, and was "in awe" of the twenty year old gold medalist who commanded the attention of the entire neighborhood. Lonnie always looked at Ali like a big brother. But, as she said in an interview:

around the time I was seventeen, I developed an enormous crush. And this may sound strange, but I knew at seventeen that someday I'd marry Muhammad.

Lonnie was an excellent student, and went on to Tennessee's prestigious Vanderbilt University. In 1982 she visited Ali in California and was shocked by his condition. "He got off the elevator and he was stumbling. He stumbled across the carpet. He wasn't speaking clearly." A friend told Lonnie that with Veronica increasingly disinterested and distanced, Ali, left to his own devices would surely die. Lonnie made the decision to move out to California where she cared for Ali while going to business school at the University of California at Los Angeles. In 1986, not long after Ali's divorce from Veronica was finalized, they married in front of twenty friends back in Louisville.

Now Ali had someone who would look out for his interests: his health, his business, and his legacy. Lonnie has a reputation for being even tougher than Hillary Clinton, but everyone—even those who disagree with her choices—is grateful that Ali finally has someone steely to balance his ever-trusting nature. As Jeremiah Shabazz said:

Lonnie is the best thing that ever happened to Ali, the absolute best. I don't care what color you are or what you believe. Anyone who cares about Muhammad has to be grateful to Lonnie.

Ali had also found a spiritual partner. Lonnie had converted to Islam, and began to fashion a new life's journey for her husband. They moved full time to Ali's farm in Berrien Springs, Michigan, and from there Ali began what he would call "the most important work of my life."

Next page: **Chicago, January 29, 1988**
Ali participates in a pro-Palestinian protest march.

I've always known that Muhammad Ali was a super sportsman; but during those hours that we were together, inside that enormous body, I saw an angel.

Hostage Harry Brill-Edwards

Previous page: **Havana, Cuba, September 10, 1998**
Ali and his wife Lonnie walk near a mural of Che Guevara during a visit to a sports center. Ali was in Cuba distributing medicines with the aid groups Direct Relief of Santa Barbara, California, and the New York-based Disarm Education Fund. Ali, who also visited Cuba in 1996, called for the end of the U.S. blockade of the island.

Left: **John F. Kennedy Airport, New York, December 4, 1990**
Ali is thanked by former hostage Harry Brill-Edwards of Ft. Lee, N.J., after returning from Iraq. In the run-up to the U.S.-led invasion of Iraq in 1991, Ali met with Iraqi president Saddam Hussein in Baghdad and succeeded in obtaining the release of 16 hostages.

Lighting the flame

Parkinson's. Depression. Isolation. In the eyes of the world, the age of Ali was over by 1989. But everyone who counted Ali out was proven dramatically wrong. It would be incorrect to say that Ali has defeated Parkinson's. That is one foe beyond his grasp. But it would also be wrong to say that Parkinson's has defeated Ali. If anything, it has allowed him to be reborn. As Ali said:

It was faith that restored my sense of purpose and my self-confidence. My faith gave me back my joy and my enthusiasm for life. I think maybe my Parkinson's is God's way of reminding me what is important: for example how we treat each other. It slowed me down and caused me to listen rather than talk. Actually people pay more attention to me now because I don't talk as much.

For decades, Ali had been generous to a fault with his name and likeness. Lonnie, Muhammad and a close circle of friends decided that it was time to reclaim his name and tell the Muhammad Ali story once again in a book. Ali would be reintroduced to a new generation of people who knew little of Vietnam beyond Hollywood or boxing beyond Mike Tyson.

To produce such a book they looked outside the circle, to a man named Thomas Hauser. Hauser was an interesting choice. An attorney as well as an author, he was best known for the book *Missing*, a scathing critique of U.S. complicity in the 1973 Military Coup in Chile. But Hauser had interviewed Ali when he was a student at Columbia University in 1967. He was a respected boxing writer and, most importantly, he demanded access to Ali and all his associates without censorship. This would not be a Hallmark card or hagiography, but a view of the man, warts and all.

Lonnie and Ali, to their credit, took a chance with Hauser and it paid off. When *Muhammad Ali: His Life and Times* hit the stores, the appetite for such a book was evident. It became a *New York Times* bestseller and reawakened interest in the champ.

Ali and Hauser went on a promotional tour, where the public for the first time was able to see, and reckon with, the Parkinson's afflicted Ali up close. This new Ali shocked many of the multitudes. At one signing stop, a woman burst into tears upon seeing him tremble up close. Ali had to kiss her cheek and say, "Don't feel bad for me. God has blessed me. I've had a good life and it's still good."

Incidents like that were difficult to endure, but Ali felt that being public with his condition was important, even if it wounded his titanic pride. As he wrote:

There are thousands of people around the world diagnosed with Parkinson's and other illnesses every day. I know a lot of them look up to me for guidance; count on me to be strong. Knowing this gives me some of the strength I need to keep going. It is one of the reasons I keep traveling, and making appearances around the world. By living my life publicly I hope to show people who are suffering from illnesses of any kind that they don't have to hide or be ashamed.

Following Hauser's book, there was a period where Ali felt he could—even in an incapacitated state—be a living symbol of peace, tolerance, and humanity. He told Hauser in 1994, "I got a plan. Someday I'm gonna hitchhike from New York to California with no money, no clothes except what I'm wearing, nothing. Then I'm going from California over to Asia, and from Asia to Europe and Africa and South America …I might even march on foot through Egypt, Israel, Lebanon, all them countries, and tell people to stop fighting and agree on a peace that's fair to everyone. Some people say that might be dangerous, but you gotta take risks…."

Ali was back, but the moment that consecrated his return to center stage, would be when NBC sports chief Dick Ebersol asked him to accept the honor of "lighting the flame" at the 1996 Summer Olympics in Atlanta. A man who came of age in the 1960s, Ebersol understood that Ali in Atlanta would make tremendous television. In the mind of Ebersol, Atlanta was the city of resurrection, which rebuilt itself after Sherman burned it to the ground during the Civil War. Atlanta was the home of Dr. Martin Luther King, Jr. and site of the King Center. During the civil rights movement Atlanta was, as President Bill Clinton said in his remarks before the Olympics, "The city too busy to hate."

Ali's own history melded perfectly with these themes. He was of course an Olympic champion who later claimed to have thrown his gold medal in the Ohio River after being denied service in a Louisville diner. And Atlanta was the city of Ali's return from boxing exile in 1970. Billy Payne, the head of Atlanta's Olympic committee didn't want a "draft dodger" lighting the flame, but Ebersol carried the day, with 3.5 billion good reasons in his corner (the money NBC had spent on rights to the games.)

Of course, Ebersol's paean to racial reconciliation didn't take into account the 10,000 African-American homeless men illegally jailed in Atlanta, or the fact that actual allies of Dr. King were outside the stadium protesting both the pre-Olympics police crackdown and destruction of public housing "necessary" to host the games. But late 20th century struggles for civil rights were not on Ebersol's brain. He wanted "must see TV" and Ali was nothing if not compelling.

It sounded great, except for one problem: Ali's Parkinson's had worsened and he didn't want to look foolish in front of the world. It almost fell through, with Billy Payne eager to tap another African-American sports legend with Atlanta roots, baseball's Henry Aaron, for the honor. But Ali couldn't resist. When his oldest friend Howard Bingham told him there would be three billion people watching, Ali got the old twinkle and agreed. In the rehearsals Ali's trembling was so bad he dropped the torch. They even developed a backup plan where 1992 swimming gold medalist Janet Evans would assist him in the actual lighting. But when his moment came, and Ali appeared from behind a curtain to the shock of the crowd, he was able to light it himself, albeit after an interminable thirty seconds where the flame seemed to refuse to ignite.

As the flames roared to life, the reaction by observers was very mixed. Ed Schuyler was furious saying, "The saddest thing I ever saw. Those pricks from TV turned him into a dancing bear." Edwin Pope said, "It should have been a moment of exaltation … instead we saw the deterioration of a man who had been a symbol of hope for his entire race." But those who wept at Ali's current state, were unable to see what he had become: a symbol of pride in the face of disease, courage in the face of infirmity, purity—down to Ali's white outfit—in an Olympic games drenched in corporate bombast. The few dissenters aside, the world united to cheer.

Shortly after I returned to America (in 1960) I had briefly lost the wonder and honor I had felt as I first put on the gold medal because I was still treated like a second class citizen in my own hometown. Now the joy of the win came flooding back to me ... In 1960, I shocked the world and won the gold medal in boxing at the Rome Olympics. In 1996 I showed the world that Parkinson's disease hadn't defeated me. I showed them I was still the greatest of all time.

Right: **Olympic Stadium, Atlanta, July 19, 1996**
Ali and President Clinton walk arm-in-arm following the opening ceremony for the Centennial Olympic Games. Ali had the honor of being the final torch bearer who lit the Olympic Flame.

Interview with Thomas Hauser

Thomas Hauser has written 33 books on subjects ranging from professional boxing to Beethoven. His first book *Missing* was nominated for the Pulitzer Prize, Bancroft Prize, and National Book Award, and was the basis for the Academy Award winning film of the same title starring Jack Lemmon and Sissy Spacek. Hauser's most celebrated work to date is *Muhammad Ali: His Life And Times,* the definitive biography of the most famous man on earth. Like *Missing*, the Ali book was nominated for a Pulitzer Prize and the National Book Award. The British edition was honored with the William Hill Book of the Year Award. Subsequently, Ali and Hauser co-authored *Healing: A Journal of Tolerance And Understanding* and criss-crossed the United States, meeting with student audiences to discuss their subject. For their efforts to combat bigotry and prejudice, they were named as co-recipients of the 1998 Haviva Reik Award. Hauser has written for *The New Yorker, The New York Times, The Times* (of London), and *The Observer.* Recently, he was retained by *The Encyclopedia Britannica* to author its entries on Muhammad Ali and Arnold Palmer. In 2005, he was honored by the Boxing Writers Association of America with the prestigious Nat Fleischer Award for "career excellence in boxing journalism."

I can't think of another writer who is so closely associated with a subject as you and Muhammad Ali. Is that a burden or a blessing?

I hadn't thought of the association in that way, but you're probably right. It's not a burden. Ali is a towering social and political figure, and my writing about him is work that I'm proud of. I don't define myself by Ali. Even in the years that I was in his inner circle, from 1988 through 1997, I never thought that my relationship with Ali defined me as a writer and certainly not as a person. But it was a joy. I don't think I'll ever have a professional experience that brings me as much joy as working on the big biography did, and I count myself very fortunate to have had that time with him. Also, it's nice to know that I'll go down in history as a footnote to the life of Muhammad Ali.

What do you mean when you speak about there being a "lost legacy" of Muhammad Ali? What is the legacy that's been lost?

Ali's history is being completely rewritten. Ali is known now to a couple of generations as being famous simply for being famous. When you look at the projects that surround him today, they are rewriting history. The Will Smith movie was a wonderful opportunity to bring the real Ali to millions of people who had no idea who he was and what he stood for, and they blew it. They completely ignored the teachings of the Nation of Islam. You could go to that movie and come out of it and think that people in the United States were prejudiced against Ali simply because he was a Muslim. That's not good history. Many people were against Ali because he adhered very vocally to what Arthur Ashe called "an American version of apartheid." He preached the doctrine that white people were created by an evil scientist with a big head named Mr. Yacub and that separation of the races was proper. On a personal level, I don't know if Ali lived what he preached in that regard any more than what he preached with regard to the treatment of women.

But Nation of Islam doctrine was eliminated from the movie and you see this white-washing of history in almost everything he does now. The idea that Muhammad Ali would go to the White House and accept a medal from George Bush at the height of the war in Iraq is very disheartening to me. But obviously, that's the road to commercial success.

What was your reaction when you heard that Ali sold an 80% interest in licensing to his name, likeness and image?
My reaction to that was that it's a continuation of this ongoing process. Now the same people who run Elvis Presley's estate will deal with Muhammad, and you know they're going to further cloud his legacy. It's a shame because Ali was so much more than image. I'm one of the people who questions the Ali Center in Louisville. I'm sure it's well-intentioned, but Ali is not about a building and a place where people go to look at pictures and sit in rooms. Ali was a spirit that lofted through the entire world before the internet. Before this whole communications revolution, he was in every one of us. He got, not just into the American psyche, but the psyche of people all over the world. Also, it's interesting that people will pay large amounts of money to be in Ali's presence.

They will pay large amounts of money for memorabilia that's somehow a unique piece of him; you know, the gloves he wore in a fight or something that he signed. His autograph is worth far more than that of any other living fighter even though he has signed millions of autographs over the years. But he hasn't been particularly successful as an endorser of products. You don't see repeat commercials with Ali like you do with other superstar athletes. Arnold Palmer gets with a product and he's there for years. Michael Jordan is there for years. Ali did a MacDonald's commercial that ran for about a week and then disappeared. The ad campaigns with Ali just don't work because Ali is not about selling products. Ali is not about licensing fees. If you taught young people today what Ali was, and still is, really about, then I think Ali would still be a strong vibrant force. But that's being eradicated and what you have instead is a blitz of commercial products.

How can young people today best learn about the real Ali?
You have to do your homework to find out who he was. Imagine what it was like living through those times when Ali was on the cutting edge of so many changes in American society and, to use his phrase, was young and handsome and fast and couldn't be beat! The only way to fully understand that is to do some historical reading and other serious research. More and more often today, we're given nonsense. And as you know, most people don't do the digging.

How do you explain that this person with a high school education who graduated near the bottom of his class was able to be ahead of the curve on the key political questions of the 1960s while the best and brightest got it wrong?
We have to be careful not to give Ali too much credit as a political and social thinker because he wasn't. In terms of the war in Vietnam I don't think he looked at the geopolitical realities of the situation and thought that the domino theory adhered to by the Johnson administration wasn't a correct foreign policy analysis. There were two things that motivated Ali to refuse induction into the United States Army. Number one, he was a 24-year-old kid who thought he'd beaten the draft because he'd be classified as 1Y. Then, all of a sudden, he's drafted. And he was a very unhappy camper, like all of us were when we thought we might be drafted. That was the first motivating force. The second was that he was acutely aware of the racial injustices in the United States. And he asked himself very

simply, "Why should I go over there and kill people in some far away country for some abstruse ideal when I can't be seated in a restaurant at home?"

A lot of us had moments of simple clarity like that. I remember in January 1968, right around the time of the Tet offensive, I was in my first year of law school. I'd gone home for intercession and was standing on the train platform in Larchmont waiting for the train to go to back to Columbia, which is where I was going to law school. It was a very cold night with a very clear sky, a lot of stars. I remember standing there saying to myself—and it could have been last week; that's how clearly I remember it—"This is absolutely nuts. What are we doing, sending people over to Vietnam to kill and be killed. For what! It makes no sense." And I think that hit Ali at some point, that the war was nuts; it was wrong. But it wasn't a thought-out process. Ali was not a political thinker. That was evident when Jimmy Carter sent him to Africa to gather support for the 1980 Summer Olympics boycott, which wound up being a humiliating experience for Muhammad and a diplomatic disaster.

Also, despite his aggressiveness in the ring, Ali was really a gentle person outside of boxing. I cannot imagine what it would have done to him to go to Vietnam and see one dead body. It would have ripped him up inside out.

What do you think about some of the revisionist histories of Ali like Sucker Punch or Mark Kram's book Ghosts of Manila?
These are two different properties. Kram was a very good writer. He had a point of view which I disagreed with, but you could have a dialogue with him and say. 'Okay, that's his point of view; he's entitled to it." But I think he was wrong when he said Ali was not an important social and political figure. That's just silly. Nelson Mandela has talked at length about what Ali meant to him while he was in

prison. As far as *Sucker Punch* is concerned, I found it an intellectually dishonest book. In the very beginning, Cashill sets up his premise by writing that Ali set himself up as a victim. No! Ali never set himself up as a victim. I defy you to find one instance when Ali set himself up as a victim. Ali refused to be a victim. Did he have sympathy for the downtrodden and oppressed? Absolutely. But you studied Ali. Can you think of a time when he set himself up as a victim?

Let me ask you; you were talking about his image today and I wanted to ask you a little bit about the $3,000 G.O.A.T book from Taschen publishers? You had an essay that was taken out.

It's significant that the book is named after Ali's corporation [G.O.A.T.], not Ali. I was a consultant to the book project in addition to writing some material that was left in and also an essay that was taken out. I was disappointed with the text in the G.O.A.T book. First, I feel they could have gotten better material to begin with. And second, once they got their material, somebody took a red pencil with a very heavy hand and started cutting. My essay, 'The Lost Legacy of Muhammad Ali' was removed from the book. I have a letter from Taschen telling me why it was removed, so I'm not speculating when I say that it wasn't Taschen's choice to remove it. There were other essays, which I thought had some very good insightful comments, that were chopped up. Some very important material was removed, and the result was a book that, forget the $3,000 and the photos and the fact that it's the size of a dinner table, not a coffee-table. If you just took the text and made it into a $14.95 paperback, there's not as much life and spark to it as there could be. And that's a shame because it was originally conceived as a very important project. The problem with all of these projects is that they're put together by people who very often don't really understand Ali. If you gave Jerry Izenberg, Bob Lipsyte, and Dave Kindred an adequate budget and told them to put together a great coffee-table photo book or documentary on Ali, they'd do something that would knock your socks off.

Do you think that's because you guys actually built that connection, that live connection to who Ali was in the 60s?

It's because we understand Ali, and that came to us in different ways. Jerry Izenberg lived through the Ali phenomenon on the scene from the beginning. I was an observer in the 1960s. I didn't have direct contact with Ali except for one moment when I met him as a college student and conducted a radio interview with him. And of course, I had considerable access later on. I think Izenberg, Lipsyte, and Kindred are all good creative artists, but it's not enough to be a creative artist. You have to understand Ali and you have to understand the Ali phenomenon, which also means understanding America at that time.

That's my next question because, to me, part of what you're saying is understanding why Ali was probably at one point the most hated prominent sports figure in the United States …

Jack Johnson was more hated.

Fair enough.

In the 60s, Ali was the most hated and most loved sports figure at the same time.

How do you explain that Ali was so hated in 1967 and, by 1974, Gerald Ford was inviting him to the White House? How did he become this symbol of reconciliation?

First, Ali is such a charming, charismatic, likeable person that it's hard to stay mad at him. There's a quote from Lloyd Wells in *Muhammad Ali: His Life and Times*: "Even the people that don't like Ali, like Ali." No matter what you thought of him, if you met him, you had to like him. Also, in the early '70s, several things changed. America began to turn against the war in Vietnam, and that cleansed one of Ali's two big sins. The first had been joining the Nation of Islam and the second was refusing induction into the United States Army. Now, all of a sudden, refusing induction into the Army didn't seem quite as bad because people started to understand that the war was wrong. Also, Ali lost to Joe Frazier; his jaw was broken by Ken Norton. And people started to feel sorry for him. They said 'I might not agree with this guy, but he does stand up for his principles.'

Then Gerald Ford became president. One of the things Ford wanted to do was heal the divisions in America, and one way of doing that was to invite Ali to the White House to say to people, "We can disagree but we can still get along." Also, Elijah Muhammad died. That came after the Ford White House trip. When Elijah died, Ali stopped spouting Nation of Islam doctrine and everybody could love him.

When Elijah Muhammad died, it seemed like Muhammad Ali almost overnight changed a lot of his public statements, indicating that he had left them in his mind, if not publicly, much earlier. Do you think he felt a sense of being in danger if he left Elijah Muhammad before '75? Dave Kindred certainly makes that point persuasively in his book *Sound and Fury*. If you go back to the early 60s, the Nation of Islam gave Ali a reason to be proud of being Black. That was very important to him. Also, Jerry Izenberg makes the point that Ali's father didn't pay much positive attention to him and Elijah Muhammad paid a lot of positive attention to him. Ali bought into the teachings of the Nation of Islam and, to the extent he might have questioned them, there was always that fear lurking in the back of his mind regarding what had happened to Malcolm. That's an area where Dave Kindred's book broke some new ground.

Let's switch gears to boxing. Can you talk a little about Ali's boxing abilities before and after exile?

I think that Ali before the exile at his peak would have beaten any heavyweight fighter at any time. He was a great fighting machine, an amazing combination of size and speed. Look at Joe Louis against Billy Conn. Billy Conn weighed 169 pounds and he was ahead on points in the 13th round. The young Ali was a great, great fighter who I don't believe Louis could have handled. All you have to do is look at the films, at what Ali was doing when he was young, and see how he could take a punch later on when he had to. The young Ali was the greatest fighter of all time. The older Ali probably peaked in Zaire and went downhill from there. I think there are a lot of fighters who could have beaten the older Ali. The Ali who fought Jimmy Young and Earnie Shavers wasn't what he'd been before. You also have to keep in mind that athletes get better as time goes on. If you took the men who won gold medals in swimming at the 1932 Olympics, they wouldn't qualify for the women's finals today. That's another reason to favor Ali over the fighters who came before him. As for those who came after, I'm not sure that fighters, unlike other athletes, have gotten better since the 60s and 70s. The conditioning techniques are better, but that's about all. The young Ali would have beaten any fighter any time.

You said Ali part-two peaked in the 1974 fight in Zaire. Do you think Ali-Frazier in Manila 1975, as great a fight as that was, was just actually two spent fighters beating hell out of each other?

I think the Joe Frazier who beat Muhammad Ali at Madison Square Garden beats Ali in Manila. And the Muhammad Ali who lost to Joe Frazier at Madison Square Garden doesn't have to go 14 rounds to knock out Frazier in Manila. They both got old. You know; one of the best moments I had with Ali was when I asked him. "If you're the Muhammad Ali in Zaire and you look across the ring and see the young Ali who fought Cleveland Williams, how do you try to fight that young guy." Usually, when I was with Ali and asked him boxing questions, he was bored by it. But I could see that this one got him going. I could see the wheels in his head turning; he really got into it. And there's that quote in *Muhammad Ali: His Life and Times* where Ali says words to the effect, "If I fought a young version of me, I would try to make rushes and tie him up and work him on the inside, but the young me would win. I was just too fast when I was young." Speed is what did it; Ali's speed was incredible. He was best when he was young.

The great boxing writer Hugh McIlvanney said 'Ali was boxing's salvation'. Was boxing in such bad shape?

Before Ali, when Sonny Liston beat Floyd Patterson, boxing had hit rock bottom in the public eye because of Liston's unsavory personality and mob connections. But then, when Ali joined the Nation of Islam and refused induction into the United States Army, sportswriters like Jimmy Cannon and Red Smith were saying, "This is the worst thing ever to happen to boxing." But whatever else could be said about Ali, he had crossover appeal. Look at Mike Tyson. People might not have liked Tyson, but they certainly knew who he was and they shelled out money to see him. When Ali was hated, people knew who he was. And when he was loved, it was even better because then you had somebody that mainstream America could root for. In that sense, Ali not only put boxing back into people's minds, he made fans out of them. There were a lot of people who couldn't have cared less about boxing as a sport, but they were rooting for Ali. He made boxing relevant again. Let's look at the times when boxing was most relevant. Boxing was relevant when John L. Sullivan was champion. He was America's first sports superstar.

Boxing was certainly relevant with Jack Johnson. Johnson turned the black-white equation in America upside down. Boxing was relevant with Jack Dempsey. He and Babe Ruth were the most famous athletes in America. People talk about Red Grange and Bill Tilden and Bobby Jones, but it was Dempsey and Ruth who were the key to the Golden Age of Sports and made sports a nation phenomenon. Boxing was obviously relevant with Joe Louis. And boxing became very relevant to what was going on in the world with Muhammad Ali. It hasn't been relevant since.

Has it not been relevant since Ali because Ali himself overshadows boxing or is it because of mismanagement of the sport?
It's not Ali's fault that boxing is no longer relevant any more than it was Joe Louis's fault when the sport diminished in relevance after him. Boxing has become a niche sport in the United States for a lot of reasons having to do with the structure of the industry. The people who run other sports understand that their competition comes from outside their arena. Football owners might compete against each other on the playing field.

But the National Football League understands that its competition is baseball, basketball, and other sports. In boxing, everybody is fighting with everyone else and cutting throats, including their own, in an attempt to get to where they want to be. Boxing is not on network television anymore, which means people are more out of touch with it. The reason it's not on network television is because the sponsors don't want to be associated with it. And boxing today is also badly run as entertainment. Boxing has always been controlled by less-than-savory elements. But in the old days, the mob understood that, to be successful, they had to have identifiable champions for the public to root for. You don't have that any more. Championships mean very little to the public today. I guarantee you that, if you go out on the street and ask a hundred people who's the heavyweight champion of the world, Mike Tyson's name will come up more than any other. People just don't know. The sport kills itself.

You have this story about Ali's attempts to be a peacemaker in 1990, going to meet with Saddam Hussein. Why do you think today he's made no effort to attempt to say anything about this very unpopular war and occupation?

I think that's a decision by the people around Ali. Muhammad is a person of pure goodwill and I think that, at the end of the day, he makes his own decisions. But he makes those decisions based on how the options are presented to him. He doesn't do independent research, so the manner in which options are presented to him dictates how he will respond.

You wrote a piece in 1993 where you speak of wanting Ali to light the Olympic flame at the 1996 Atlanta Olympics. You put that forward and, after he did it, you had mixed feelings about it.

I didn't have mixed feelings about his doing it. I think it was wonderful that he lit the Olympic flame in Atlanta. It was the best thing in the world that could have happened at those games. What I'm disappointed with is that lighting the Olympic flame gave Ali an extraordinary platform to stand upon in advancing a whole new round of initiatives. And instead of using that platform primarily to advance an agenda of tolerance and understanding, it was used for economic gain. I don't think that was all Ali's doing. I think he made most of the final decisions, but those decisions were based on how the options were presented to him.

By Lonnie? By a coterie of business people?

Lonnie is certainly the most influential person in Muhammad's life in that regard. There are others who also have influence.

How did you feel when you saw him get the Presidential Medal of Freedom from George Bush?

I was very disappointed because all Muhammad Ali would have to do is say two words about the war in Iraq: "It's wrong." That wouldn't dictate what people think, but it would dictate what a lot of people think about. It would have political commentators talking. It would draw more analogies between this war and the war in Vietnam.

It would also force them to talk about the real Ali in the 1960s.

Instead he goes to the White House and plays these little games with George Bush and that photo goes out on the wire services. I thought it was unfortunate. In *The Lost Legacy of Muhammad Ali*, I wrote about December 31, 1999, when Ali rang the bell at the New York Stock Exchange. That's not where the young Ali would have been on a day of symbolic importance like that. The young Ali would have been some place like a homeless shelter or a soup kitchen bringing hope to people. Larry Merchant, who I'm very fond of, suggested to me that the young Ali might have been in bed with Halle Berry. But he wouldn't have been at the New York Stock Exchange. And I'll tell you something else. After Hurricane Katrina, I think Ali should have been in the Superdome. If Ali had been in the Superdome after Hurricane Katrina, it would have brought hope and joy to all of the people who were undergoing a horrible, horrible experience. I mean, think about it. You've just lost your home. Think about it! If you went home and everything was burned down to the ground and you had nothing. No books, no clothes, your work product has all been lost. And it's not just you, it's the whole city; everything is gone. Then they put you in a stadium, where there's very little food and inadequate sanitation. If you're there and Muhammad Ali, as debilitated as he is, were there; if he was going around hugging every person in the stadium, it would give some hope and some joy and something good would have come out of that horrible experience. It also would have drawn a lot of attention in a different way to the mishandling of the situation by the federal government. Ali's presence would have drawn a stark contrast between real compassion and what we've got in Washington today. That's where Ali should have been, and he wasn't. And don't tell me his health wouldn't have allowed it because, if he can go to Germany for a six-figure appearance, he could have been there.

You think that it's a case of his not being presented with the option?
You know enough about Ali. If somebody had said what I just said to you and asked him, "Do you want to go to the Superdome," do you think he would have said no?

When was the last time you had contact with him?
I haven't seen him in a long time. I think 1999 was the last time.

Do you miss him?
That's a good question. Ali was a source of joy in my life, I enjoyed the time I was with him. It's a wonderful memory in the time capsule of life for me. I'm not sure how much joy I would derive from spending time with Ali today, given the climate around him and the way options are being presented to him. We had what I felt was a very direct, honest relationship. I'm happy with the way things were, and I'm content with the way things are today. I'm happy with the time I spent with Ali, and I'm proud about what I've written about him. It's nice to know that, a hundred years from now, if somebody wants to know about Ali, they're going to read my books. And for serious scholars like yourself, I'll always have a hand in shaping Ali's legacy. I wouldn't change my experience with him, and I only wish him the best. On top of everything the public sees and on top of Ali being a great athlete and a very important social and political figure, he's a very, very, very nice man. That was one of the things that always struck me when I was with him; and it's one of the reasons that I still smile whenever I think of him.

Maybe I was great in the ring, but outside of boxing, I'm just a brother like other people.
I want to live a good life, serve God, help everybody I can. And one more thing. I'm still gonna find out who stole my bike when I was 12 years old in Louisville and I'm gonna whup him. That was a good bike.

Right: **Hamburg, Germany, November 27, 2003**
Ali, with his wife Lonnie, jokes with the audience while accepting the Millennium Bambi 2003 media award for lifetime achievement.

I always liked to chase the girls. Parkinson's stops all that. Now I might have a chance to go to heaven.

Left: **Harlem, New York, December 1, 2004**
Ali and his daughter Hana Ali pose as they arrive to promote Ali's latest book, *The Soul Of A Butterfly,* co-authored with Hana. In the book Ali discusses his experience of living with Parkinson's.

Bushwhacked

On November 9, 2005 U.S. President George W. Bush, in the face of mounting opposition to his war agenda for the Middle East, took the time to hand a medal around the slack, immobile neck of former heavyweight boxing champion—and the most famous war resister in U.S history—Muhammad Ali.

Ali was one of a bevy of recipients of the Presidential Medal of Freedom at a White House ceremony. While Karl Rove and Donald Rumsfeld chuckled behind him, Bush said:

Only a few athletes are ever known as the greatest in their sport, or in their time. But when you say, 'The Greatest of All Time' is in the room, everyone knows who you mean. It's quite a claim to make, but as Muhammad Ali once said, 'It's not bragging if you can back it up.' And this man backed it up … The real mystery, I guess, is how he stayed so pretty. [Laughter.] It probably had to do with his beautiful soul. He was a fierce fighter and he's a man of peace.

Watching the ceremony, it was heartbreaking to see Bush, a chicken-hearted man of empire, bathe himself in Ali's aura and rhapsodize about "peace." To see the once-indomitable Ali, besieged by Parkinson's, eyes filmed over, hands shaking, led around by a self-described "War President" was horrifying.

About the only thing Bush and Ali have in common is that they both moved mountains to stay out of Vietnam. The difference, of course, was that while Ali sacrificed his title and risked years in

White House, Washington D.C., November 9, 2005

nt George W. Bush presents Ali with the Presidential Medal of Freedom.

Federal prison, Bush joined the country club otherwise known as the Texas National Guard, showing up for duty every time he had a dentist appointment.

But the Champ still had one last rope-a-dope up his sleeve. As a playful Bush moved in front of Ali, he apparently thought it would be cute to put up his fists in a boxing stance. Ali leaned back and made a circular motion around his temple, as if the President must be crazy to want to tangle with him even now.

This moment recalled the Ali of many years ago who was not so beloved, so cuddly, so harmless. This was a fleeting glimpse of the Ali who once was able to say things that would have made John Ashcroft demand a federally funded exorcism. This was the Ali who publicly allied himself with the Nation of Islam and announced, "I ain't no Christian."

Back then, Ali could level criticism about an ill-advised, unfair war in Vietnam, with the that unforgettable headline-grabbing statement of his "I ain't got no quarrel with the Vietcong ... no VietCong ever called me nigger." And he elaborated that even further: "I ain't going no 10,000 miles to help murder and kill other poor people. If I want to die, I'll die right here, right now, fightin' you, if I want to die. You my enemy, not no Chinese, no Vietcong, no Japanese. You my opposer when I want freedom. You my opposer when I want justice. You my opposer when I want equality. Want me to go somewhere and fight for you? You won't even stand up for me right here in America, for my rights and my religious beliefs. You won't even stand up for my right here at home."

If Ali had said things like that today about our current war, it would have earned him, not a medal, but a one-way trip to Guantánamo prison.

Perhaps a far more fitting and true tribute to Ali was on display at an antiwar demonstration in 2006, where an older woman of African descent, evoking the horrors of the aftermath of Hurricane Katrina, held up a sign that read simply, "No Iraqi ever left me to die on a roof." This was a direct reference to a quote attributed to Ali that "no Vietnamese ever called me 'nigger.'

Both statements in a few short words encompass both the anger and internationalism so needed today. These are statements not of pacifism but of the struggle to end war. This is the Ali that they can never bury—not even under the pall of devastating illness and a mountain of cheap medals.

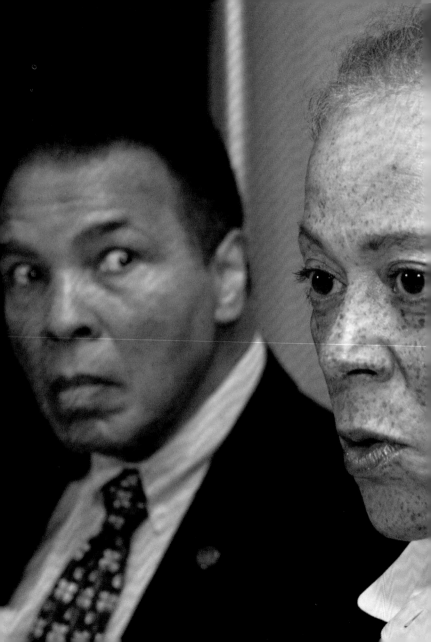

We believe in the governor and the agenda that she has for the state.

Lonnie Ali

Left: **Detroit, October 4, 2006**

Ali listens to his wife, Lonnie, speak during a news conference in support of Michigan Governor Jennifer Granholm's bid for re-election, citing her efforts to overturn Michigan's ban on embryonic stem cell research, an issue close to their hearts. They had previously campaigned with Governor Granholm when she was first elected in 2002.

Interview with Mike Marqusee

Mike Marqusee is the author of *Redemption Song: Muhammad Ali and the Spirit of the 1960s.* **The book was short-listed for the William Hill Sports Book of the Year award and was voted one of twenty-five 'Books to Remember' from 1999 by the New York Public Library. It is also included in the Sports Pages Bookshop list of the thirty best sports books ever published. A new edition of** *Redemption Song,* **with an afterword on Muhammad Ali and the war on terror, was published in June 2005.**

Your book is titled Redemption Song. *Do you see Ali as someone who either requires redemption or was redeemed? Please explain the title.*
In Bob Marley's lyric, the "redemption songs" are the residue of suffering and oppression. By giving a body to that historical experience, to the struggles to survive and to overcome, they offer, however fleetingly, a sense of "redemption." What's redeemed is the suffering and the sacrifice. In my book (as in Marley's song) the

specific reference is, of course, to the struggle of the African Diaspora, especially in north America, and more broadly the global struggle against racism and colonialism. "Redemption songs" contain the seed of resistance, and no movement of resistance flourishes without them. They're songs of hope, sometimes of triumph, profoundly tinged with the living memory of pain. The title also refers to Ali himself: the arc of his story, and the way that story has been purloined by an establishment still fearful of its real import. In Ali's story, as in Malcolm X's, a victim of white supremacy is "redeemed" by the encounter with the Nation of Islam and radical black consciousness. In Ali's moment of triumph in Kinshasa, what was "redeemed" were the sacrifices he had made for his principles. Kinshasa was a great fight, but because of its historical context, it was also like a song—a concentrated lyrical expression that lodged in the popular memory.

Ali was clearly someone angered, incensed, by racism in U.S. society. Why do you think he chose the separatist Black Nationalism of the Nation of Islam as opposed to the marching, and sitting-in integration politics of Dr. Martin Luther King?

As a young black man in a racist society trying to make his way in a decidedly dubious industry Cassius Clay was looking first and foremost for a strategy of survival and self-advancement. But unlike his predecessors of previous generations, he was no longer willing or indeed able to adopt the traditional model of subservience and servility. Even in the early sixties, the integrationist rhetoric of the civil rights leaders grated in the ears of many young black people, who wanted equality and rights, on their own terms, not just permission to enter white society. The Nation offered Clay a pride in himself and his people not dependent on white approbation. It was a prominent and accessible form of militant, defiant black solidarity that at the same time generally avoided political or practical resistance to racism.

This political abstentionism (which accompanied the separatism) provided protection from the very real dangers of direct conflict with white authorities. One of the ironies of Ali's career is that his choice of political abstentionism, his search for a space where he could avoid conflict with white authorities, brought him into direct, prolonged conflict with those authorities, in the boxing world and far beyond.

In your book you make a very interesting parallel between Ali and Bob Dylan. Can you speak about that? Why is it helpful to compare a Hibbing, Minnesota folkie who hated the press with a heavyweight boxer who loved the spotlight?

Ali and Dylan were the same age, brought up on much of the same TV and pop music, exposed to the same big historical events and tides. Both were exceptional and irreducible individuals who nonetheless were profoundly shaped by the events of their time. The student sit-ins of the early sixties unleashed a wave of political and cultural dissent, and imbued a section of young people of the era with an extraordinary self-confidence—a headlong, sometimes reckless challenge to conventions, political, social, and aesthetic.

Without the grassroots African-American freedom struggle of the early sixties, Cassius Clay never would have become Muhammad Ali, and Robert Zimmerman would never have become Bob Dylan (not just the name change, but the whole package). Ali and Dylan were also among the earliest to experience the cult of youth celebrity in the TV age—and both of them waged a ferocious contest to reclaim their identities from the media. Of course, they adopted radically different approaches to this. Dylan sneered at, then turned his back on the media ("something is happening but you don't know what it is"). Ali mixed charm, wit, effervescence with his defiance and his often startlingly radical critique of U.S. political and social assumptions. Because of their achievements and extraordinary personalities, Dylan and Ali helped make the study of popular culture respectable. But the comparison is also important because of the critical differences it highlights. Not only between a boxer and a singer-songwriter, but between black and white. In challenging authority, Ali confronted levels of hatred and danger Dylan could only imagine (and which he did spend time imagining, as reflected in all those wonderfully paranoid lyrics in "It's alright Ma" or "Maggie's Farm" or "Memphis Blues Again".)

There are writers today who criticize Ali for "turning his back" on Malcolm X, which seems like a very heavy criticism for a 22-year-old boxer. What do you say to that?

I think it's an unreal criticism to make of a 22-year-old, whether a boxer or a post-grad student. After all, who didn't turn their backs on Malcolm X? The bulk of the membership of The Nation, the civil rights movement leaders, the white media (which covered Malcolm's murder as retribution for the preacher of hate). Malcolm himself urged his followers not to be hard on Ali, whose autonomy he always respected.

Ali came out against the Vietnam war at a time when the—soon to be gigantic—movement was barely a wisp. If we agree that he couldn't tell the future, how can we understand his foresight?

I don't think it was foresight. One of the things that makes his stand so astounding, and so inspiring, is that nobody foresaw, in 1966, that protest against the war would grow into a global deluge. Ali was told by everyone that his stance would isolate him, and he had no reason to disbelieve them. When he defied the draft, he had no reason whatsoever to think that it would ultimately win him popularity and accolades, as opposed to condemnation, prison and poverty. But he did have two guideposts that others lacked. First, a living inheritance of black antagonism to white men's wars, from Elijah Muhammad and Malcolm X as well as [Paul] Robeson and [W.E.B.] DuBois. And second, a living connection to a social constituency that was already feeling the sharp end of the war—the black working class—whose members were from the outset more skeptical about the war's aims and costs than their white counterparts. Ali had a powerful sense of accountability to his community, and it was this sense that often steered him when other factors were muddled.

Why was the Ali of the 1970s so remarkably less political than the Ali of the 1960s? Other athletes like Jim Brown didn't suffer a similar slide. In the course of the decade, the African-American freedom movement fragmented, receded, and declined. Ali's fortunes were always bound up with its rhythms. His great moment of vindication in Kinshasa coincided with the downfall of Nixon and the end of the Vietnam War. He was welcomed into the fold as an icon of conciliation, a way of letting the bygones of the sixties be bygones. Ali's political actions were almost always undertaken as an individual but they acquired tremendous symbolic currency. The thing about symbols, however, is that in different contexts they take on different meanings. I also suspect that Ali was exhausted by his years of resistance and hoped to recoup, financially at least, some of the sacrifices he had made. Though he was profoundly shaped by ideas, he was never driven by political ideology the way Jim Brown was. Ali was only one of a number of 60s icons of rebellion who made their peace with the status quo in those years (Dylan, for example, turned to fundamentalist Christianity in 1979).

What were your thoughts seeing Ali given the Presidential Medal Of Freedom by Bush?
I suppose it's something like I feel when I see Dylan making a deal

with Starbucks. It's no longer in the least surprising but it's worth pausing for a moment to absorb the irony. Of course, I'd have liked to see Ali throw the medal back in Bush's face, but any prospect of that happening evaporated years ago. In a way, it's a perverse tribute to the power of Ali's stand in the 1960s that the current generation of warmongers are so keen to be associated with him. But it's also an indication that Ali has completely lost touch with the grassroots.

What did you think of the movie "Ali"?

I was amazed that one of the most exciting narratives of the 20th century could be turned into such a boring movie. It's not just that Will Smith plays Ali with a solemnity and sense of farseeing purpose entirely alien to the real Ali; it's that the movie is like a series of edifying tableaux, illustrating a straightforward progress through trial to triumph. Then there are the small but significant political ellipses. The account of Malcolm's break with The Nation leaves out the "chickens coming home to roost" comment and its fallout. It's implied that in joining the Nation of Islam Ali became a "Muslim" in the familiar sense, and the audience is spared the full Nation of Islam menu, and indeed the full fury of a white-bating Malcolm. In its recreation of the sights and sounds of the era, the film is remarkable: but it's too sentimental about both Ali and his politics.

Lastly, why is the memory of the Ali of the 1960s still relevant today?

The challenges Ali wrestled with are clearly with us today: U.S. military and imperial power, the tension between individual conscience and legal duty to the state, racism and the relation of Islam and the west, the possibilities and difficulties of using popular culture to disseminate dissident ideas. Above all, Ali's story—with all its contradictions—is a reminder that resistance comes in unexpected forms, from unexpected sources, and that the apparently powerless do sometimes succeed in turning the tables on the powerful.

chapter 7

Ali: Legend and icon

Ali's cultural legacy

Muhammad Ali is that most peculiar of icons: someone who inspires the tall tales and gilded truths of a Paul Bunyan or John Henry yet, unlike his fellow superheroes, lives and breathes among us. In a sense, the Ali of folklore has long since passed. The Ali of yesteryear, the "dragonslayer" of Gerald Early's youth, is as gone as Sam Cooke, Martin Luther King, or Malcolm X. The "Louisville Lip" is no more, but the persistence of Ali is nonetheless remarkable.

Despite his public incapacitation, he doesn't evoke pity as much as curiosity and exploration. He is an iconic figure who is welcomed to the company of other famous people. Since Ali can't tell us how great he is anymore, the mass culture insists on doing it for him. More than 800 sports books either entirely about Ali or that use Ali as part of their central thesis have been published in countless languages. They are cut to fit every taste from serious academic texts to comic books (in my hands right now I hold a collectors' copy of the *Superman vs. Muhammad Ali* comic.) Most bombastically, Taschen Books issued G.O.A.T. (Greatest of All Time), the coffee table book which is the size of a coffee table and costs as much as a mid-sized sedan.

Previous page: **Award at Planet Hollywood, Las Vegas, April 21, 1995**
The bronze of Ali was made by world renowned sports sculptor John Petek, of Billings, Montana.
Right: **New York, January 31, 1978**
Ali at a press conference plugging a comic book in which he beats Superman.

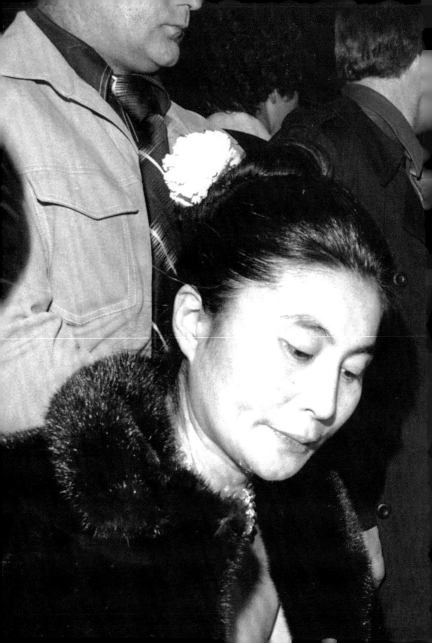

Many despair at all the evil and unrest and disorder in the world today ... but I see a new social order and I see the dawn of a new day.

Coretta Scott King

Previous page: **Kennedy Center for the Performing Arts, Washington, D.C., January 20, 1977**
Ali, with John Lennon and his wife Yoko Ono, attends the gala honoring President-elect Jimmy Carter on the eve of his inauguration.
Right: **Atlanta, Georgia, January 10, 1986**
Ali embraces Coretta Scott King, the widow of the Rev. Martin Luther King, Jr., at a news conference launching a celebration for the first national holiday honoring the slain civil rights leader.

He didn't believe a woman's place was in the ring, but he can appreciate it when he sees we can do it, same way men can do it.

Laila Ali

Previous page: **New York, January 20, 1992**
The eighth annual Congress of Racial Equality (CORE) Martin Luther King dinner. From left to right: CORE national chairman Roy Innis, movie director Oliver Stone, Muhammad Ali and actor Anthony Quinn.

Right: **Aladdin Hotel, Las Vegas, Nevada, August 18, 2002**
Laila Ali poses with her father after beating Suzy Taylor to win the IBA Super Middleweight title. Laila is the only one of Ali's children who has followed him into boxing. His youngest child, by Veronica Porche, she made her pro début in 1999. An undisputed champion of women's boxing, she has won all three major women's championship belts, and is the most famous women's professional boxer in the world She has written a self-help book called *Reach!* and has been pictured in glamorous features for magazines such as *Ebony, Cosmopolitan* and *Marie Claire.*

Muhammad Ali is quite possibly the most recognized sports figure of our time ... That's why we are especially proud to recognize him on our box during our 75th anniversary celebration.

Wheaties market manager Jim Murphy

Left: **New York, February 4, 1999**

Ali poses next to a Wheaties "The Breakfast of Champions" poster during the unveiling of the 75th Anniversary cereal box in his honor.

Next page: **Los Angeles, August 4, 2000**

Ali's boxing shoes from the first Ali-Frazier fight in March 8, 1971 sit on display at Butterfield's & Butterfield's, an eBay company, waiting to be auctioned off. The starting bid was expected to be between $100,000 and $150,000.

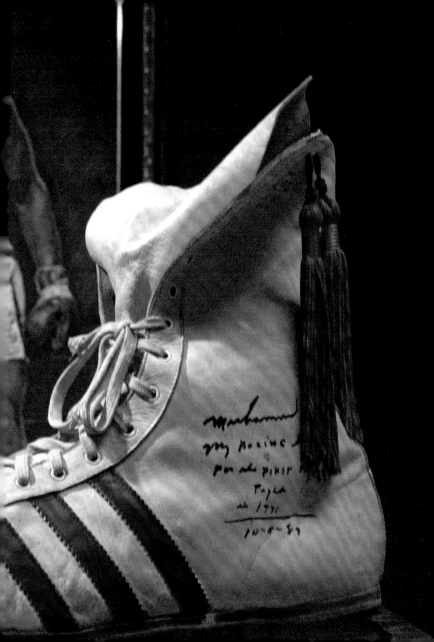

Muhammad Ali—the movie

In 2001, Hollywood—never wishing to be left out of the hype—entered the fray with the big-budget film *Ali*. It was released with tremendous hype and high expectations, boasting an all-star cast that included Will Smith as Ali and Jon Voight as Howard Cosell, and was directed by Michael Mann.

The film failed to match expectations either critically or at the box office. Boxing and sports historians attacked *Ali* for presenting its subject as a one-dimensional saint with his ideas fully formed. Artistically, despite game performances from Messrs. Smith and Voight, which garnered them both Oscar nominations, a constant critique was that the film failed to match the kinetic energy of the man himself.

In other words, nobody—not even the Fresh Prince—could ever do as good a job playing Ali as Ali himself. As Roger Ebert said, "[*Ali*] lacks much of the flash, fire and humor of Muhammad Ali and is shot more in the tone of a eulogy than a celebration."

Right: **Grauman's Chinese Theater, Hollywood, Los Angeles, December. 12, 2001**
Ali and Will Smith give each other pretend jabs at the première of the movie *Ali*. Smith portrays Ali in the movie. Also pictured is Smith's son Trey.

The Muhammad Ali Center

The disappointing box office for the movie *Ali* did little to slow the grandest demonstration of Ali's cultural endurance: the opening in 2005 of the $75 million Muhammad Ali Center in Louisville. The aspirations of the center are no less outsized than those dreamed of by the 18-year old "Mayor of Olympic Village" himself, so many years ago. The Center's mission statement proclaims:

Serving as an international education and cultural center that is inspired by the ideals of its visionary founder Muhammad Ali, the Muhammad Ali Center is a place to explore the greatness that lies within you and find the inspiration to pursue your potential. The Ali Center's innovative and immersive visitor experience, public programming, and global initiatives carry on Muhammad's legacy and continue his life's work. Much more than a place that tells the story of one man's journey, the Ali Center reaches beyond its physical walls to promote respect, hope and understanding and to inspire adults and children everywhere to be as great as they can be.

Yet even the Center has been criticized—in a similar vein as the film—for not measuring up to the man. As his biographer Thomas Hauser said in our interview, "I'm one of the people who questions the Ali Center in Louisville. I'm sure it's well-intentioned, but Ali is not about a building and a place where people go to look at pictures and sit in rooms. Ali was a spirit that lofted through the entire world before the internet. Before this whole communications revolution, he was in every one of us. He got, not just into the American psyche, but the psyche of people all over the world."

Perhaps this is the ultimate irony of iconography in the age of mass-media. Efforts to market, package, and project your own image will invariably be tripped up by the fact that people have their own perceptions and memories that resist the hidden hand of the market. In other words, Ali's spirit is so precious to people, they don't want or need movies or museums to commune with. They have the man himself in their mind's eye. It's a dilemma the young Ali would have found hilarious, and one Ali inc. undoubtedly finds endlessly frustrating.

Next page: **Louisville, Kentucky, June 30, 2003**
Ali stands next to the model of the Muhammad Ali Center. The museum celebrating the life of one of the 20th century's most recognizable figures opened in November 2005.

Interview with Etan Thomas

Few athletes embody the legacy of Muhammad Ali like the National Basketball Association's Etan Thomas. Thomas is known in the world of professional sports as the Center/Power Forward for the Washington Wizards. Yet he is rapidly gaining a reputation in the worlds of poetry and politics. His book of poems *More Than An Athlete* has been an underground sensation in the United States. He has also been an outspoken opponent of the wars both abroad and at home. Thomas electrified anti-war Washington in September 2005 when he delivered a withering poem about the Bush administration in front of thousands of protestors. In addition, Thomas is a courageous spokesperson against the death penalty and the system of capital punishment. Here we speak to Thomas about Ali's legacy and the current political situation.

Let's start with the big question. What does Muhammad Ali's legacy mean to you?

What Muhammad Ali's Legacy means to me … When talking about Muhammad Ali, it is important to remember that all of these people in mainstream America, who now look at him with reverence and dignity did not feel that way when he was in his prime. It is important to remember that he was one of the most vilified and reviled men at the time. When he made the decision not to enter his name in the draft, not to step forward and fight in a war that he did not agree in, he was looked upon with hate. All of the people who once cheered him and marveled at his ability and overall skills in the ring, looked upon him with eyes of contempt. As if to say how dare he not jump at the opportunity to fight for his country. But the reality was, that he was the epitome of standing up for what you believed in. For having the moral courage to ignore public opinion and stand on his convictions. You have to remember that this was a different time. A time where Black People all over the country were being brutally lynched, burned alive, doused with water hoses, and attacked with dogs, and this is by the police. This was a time of dire consequences for such actions, and a proud Black Man as Muhammad Ali who waited until he won the belt, until he was the heavyweight champion of the world, to say to the entire country, "I gotcha. This is who I am. And I'm not going to give you any choice but to accept me as man. You can't put me in a box no matter if you want to or not." Muhammad Ali is the symbol for self-pride and dignity. For knowledge of self and knowing your destiny on this earth. This is who I looked upon—along with Bill Russell, John Carlos and Tommy Smith, Jim Brown etc—as role models. The athletes that I aspired to emulate as far as having the courage to stand up for what you believe in.

For me to be compared to any of them is definitely a compliment and I am honored to draw that comparison, but it is not one that I would make. They are the pioneers, I am just trying to follow in their footsteps, but I particularly don't like the comparisons although I am very honored by them. I feel that there can never be another Muhammad Ali, there is only one. Nobody else has the capability of being on that level.

Muhammad Ali paid a very heavy price for coming out against the war in Vietnam. I know for a fact many athletes today oppose the war and occupation of Iraq. Why don't more athletes protest today like they did in the 1960s? I know you get that question a lot. Can you detail some of the criticism you have encountered?

Of course everyone is not going to agree with you, and of course you are going to receive mountains of criticism from every direction. The first thing the right wing media does is try to either discredit, ridicule, or vilify anyone who speaks out against mainstream America or the ideologies or policies of mainstream America whether they are the injustices of racism, an unjust war, or an inadequate, unqualified, poor excuse for a president of the United States. They want to discredit you to the point that anything that you say becomes obsolete and easily dismissed. After I spoke at the September 2005 anti-war rally in DC, I received an enormous amount of praise and criticism. While some sang praises others were appalled. Which was to be expected. I don't have a problem with anyone disagreeing with me, most right wing conservative Republicans do, but don't try to discredit me as if I don't know what I am talking about, just because I don't share your blind view of following along with every bad decision the Bush administration makes. There were even people who created these sites on the internet showing these poems that aren't mine, and then criticizing the poems that I did not write only in an attempt to discredit me. To try to show anyone who wanted to listen to me that I did not know what I was talking about. This is the type of strategy usually seen every night on the Bill O'Reilly show or Hannity and Colmes. Whenever there is an opposing viewpoint, they either ridicule, discredit, vilify, or demean the person in an effort to make anything they say after that become obsolete. They are very crafty I have to give them that.

Why don't more athletes speak out today compared to the 1960s?
I always get this question, and I have to always answer it the same way. I can only speak for myself. I personally choose to speak out because that is my passion, but I in no way expect it to be everyone else's passion as well. That would simply not be fair of me to say. I do believe that just as athletes should have the right to speak out, they should also have the right not to. I don't feel that it is fair to label anyone a "slave" as [*New York Times*] sports columnist William Rhoden did in his book *40 Million Dollar Slaves,* just because they are not the type of athlete that he would want them to be. I do wish that more athletes would speak out, but I don't feel that they are obligated to do so. What if they are simply not into politics? Can't they have the freedom to just be themselves? You are a public figure, but that does not mean that you are public domain, and it is important to understand the difference.

Muhammad Ali always had a very strong, but very basic critique of the war in Vietnam, with statements like, "I ain't got no quarrel with them Vietcong." You have a more intense critique of the current war in Iraq. Can you share that?
It's interesting because now you are beginning to hear some Republicans saying, "Hey maybe this war wasn't such a great idea. Maybe we should have had an exit strategy in place before we invaded the country."

Now, in the wake of a civil war they are saying, maybe we should have thought this whole thing through a little better. John McCain recently was on "Meet The Press" and said in essence that he would have done everything differently. He explained that he would have paid more attention to the actual exit strategy, that he does not have confidence in Rumsfeld, he even acknowledges that we did not have enough troops from the beginning to successfully win in Iraq but somehow still claimed to have this blind faith in the Bush administration's decision making skills. I just don't understand it.

He says that he will still support Bush because mistakes are made in every war. Understands that us losing in Iraq would be catastrophic but at the same time somehow still supports Bush. The reality is that we don't have additional troops available to send to Iraq, which is what McCain said will be the only way we can be successful there, and Colin Powell said we would need before this entire invasion took place, but that's a whole other story. They keep using these talking points of we'll stand down when the Iraqis stand up, kind of dangling the carrot of troop reduction because that is what the entire country is calling for. But this entire strategy of the Bush administration was flawed and inadequate.

There is no exit strategy, they can say what they want, there is no way that we can "adapt to win" as [Republican National Committee leader] Ken Mehlman says, and at the same time bring our troops home. It just isn't possible. They got us into this mess and they should finish it. Not leave it for the next president, which is what's probably going to happen anyway. They keep accusing the Democrats of supporting a cut and run philosophy, but the Bush administration are the ones who cut and ran from Osama Bin Laden after 9/11, and simply focused their attention on the wrong person. However, anyone with eyes can see that this was a bad idea, but you would be amazed at the hate mail I received. People who said that I wasn't American because I didn't support "our President." That I was somehow unpatriotic, which couldn't be further from the truth. I think that what's really unpatriotic is sitting by and allowing a president to make bad decision after bad decision and not say anything about it. Iraq will go down in history as an American tragedy, and people will ask why didn't anyone do anything, how did they let this happen? Little kids will be reading about it in their text books about all of the lives lost, innocent Iraqi civilians slaughtered, American soldiers killed, and wonder what type of patriotism did all of those people have who went along with this show.

Interview with Lester Rodney

MARYLAND MAY 2006

Lester Rodney was the legendary sports editor of the *Daily Worker* **in the 1930s. Now 97 years old, he is the last remaining sportswriter to have covered the epoch-marking 1938 rematch when the Black American boxer Joe Louis dealt a mighty blow to Hitler's Germany by defeating the German Max Schmeling. Here are three questions I put to the great writer.**

Archie Moore once said that he believed Ali would defeat Joe Louis in four out of five fights. As someone who covered Joe Louis, what do you think of this?

Picking the winner in mythical fights between men of a different era is always subjective (and probably generational.) I have great respect for Ali, who I only saw on TV a few times, but I have to think that Louis, who threw the hardest and fastest punches of anyone (including Johnson and Dempsey) would have caught up to him. Sue me.

How do you compare the social impact of Joe Louis to Ali?
Louis was a person of his times, well before the civil rights campaign and the Black Power era. He was not an outspoken fighter for rights the way Jackie R. and Ali were (and the Army used him in World War II to try to hide the racist realities confronting black soldiers.) In the 1930s, he did not have to be recognizably militant to have an electrifying, transforming effect. His defeat of the best representatives of the white race in the uniquely man-to-man sport was enough. Blacks didn't care that he avoided "offending white sensibilities" outside the ring. They understood that.

Yet he was not, as sometimes portrayed, just a passive, non-conscious medium. He gradually realized what he meant to his people and in his own way acted upon that, particularly during the war years, when he helped end some of the more blatant racism at Fort Bragg, N.C. And I heard him in the dressing room after the 1938 Schmeling fight expressing (in his own way) his feelings about beating the man who Hitler had endowed with the white man's superiority over the *untermensch*.

Anyhow, to answer your question, Joe and Ali were very different types in different social eras. I appreciated both of them differently.

As someone who lost employment and was persecuted in the age of McCarthyism, what did it mean to you when Ali burst onto the scene?
It was like a bolt of blue after a very long night. Ali helped wake up a nation. Of course I was thrilled and ecstatic when Ali told them to shove the Vietnam war. I thought "No Vietcong ever called me a nigger" was classic.

Photo Credits

All photographs (including cover) courtesy of EMPICS

Quotation Credits

CHAPTER 1

p13 http://www.brownhotel.com
p18 Thomas Hauser, *Muhammad Ali: His Life and Times,* p19 (Hereafter referred to as Hauser)
p25 Hauser, p16
p30 Hauser, p14
p35 Hauser p17

CHAPTER 2

p45 Mike Marqusee, *Redemption Song: Muhammad Ali And the Spirit of the Sixties,* p48 (Hereafter referred to as Marqusee
p52 Hauser, p41
p56 Dave Kindred, *Sound and Fury, Two Powerful Lives, One Fateful Friendship,* p36 (Hereafter referred to as Kindred)
p63 Hauser, p49
p66 http://www.boxing-memorabilia.com/Muhammad_Ali_Quotes_2.htm
p70 Hauser, p39
p73 documentary, "Muhammad Ali: Through the Eyes of the World"
p75 http://www.newstatesman.co.uk/199906280042.htm

CHAPTER 3

p83 http://observer.guardian.co.uk/omm/story/0,,1132404,00.html
p92 http://www.boxing-memorabilia.com/Muhammad_Ali_Quotes_2.htm
p103 "A Change is Gonna Come" Lyrics by Sam Cooke
p107 http://observer.guardian.co.uk/osm/story/0,,1072751,00.html
p121 Marqusee, p140
p125 Marqusee, p130
p135 http://www.usatoday.com/sports/century/alifs01.htm
p136, Marqusee, p141

CHAPTER 4

p153 Kindred, p94
p154 http://www.boxing-memorabilia.com/Muhammad_Ali_Quotes_2.htm
p157 http://www.boxing-memorabilia.com/Muhammad_Ali_Quotes_2.htm
p159 http://www.boxing-memorabilia.com/Muhammad_Ali_Quotes_2.htm
p161 http://www.boxing-memorabilia.com/Muhammad_Ali_Quotes_2.htm
p163 http://www.boxing-memorabilia.com/Muhammad_Ali_Quotes_2.htm

164, Hauser, p160
167 http://www.worldofquotes.com/author/ Muhammad-Ali/1/index.html
170 Hauser, p184
176 Hauser, p189
183 http://www.boxing-memorabilia.com/Muhammad_Ali_Quotes_2.htm
187 Empics.com reporter's caption
195 Hauser, p173

CHAPTER 5

227 *Boxing Classics—The Muhammad Ali v Joe Frazier Trilogy—1971-1975*
231 http://www.sportingnews.com/archives/sports2000/moments/141892.html
234 http://www.boxing-memorabilia.com/Muhammad_Ali_Quotes_2.htm
239 http://www.boxing-memorabilia.com/Muhammad_Ali_Quotes_2.htm
240 http:// archives.tcm.ie/businesspost/2002/08/04/story437381628.asp
245 http://www.amazon.com/Big-Fight-Muhammad-Blue-Lewis/dp/0224063065
p249 http://espn.go.com/sportscentury/features/00242468.htmll
p250 http://www.boxing-memorabilia.com/Muhammad_Ali_Quotes_2.htm
p253 http://www.boxing-memorabilia.com/Muhammad_Ali_Quotes_2.htm
p254 http://www.guardian.co.uk/ netnotes/ article/0,,635130,00.html
p257 http://einsiders.com/reviews/archives/show_theatrical.php?review_theatricle=45
p258 http://www.boxing-memorabilia.com/Muhammad_Ali_Quotes_2.htm
p265 http://www.boxing-memorabilia.com/Muhammad_Ali_Quotes_2.htm
p266 Norman Mailer, in the documentary, *When We Were Kings*
p277 Hauser, p500
p278 Kindred, p207
p285 http://sportsillustrated.cnn.com/centurys_best/news/1999/05/05/thrilla_manila/

CHAPTER 6

p317 Kindred, p214
p321 Hauser, p356
p331 http://www.secondsout.com/usa/colhauser.cfm?ccs=208&cs=20115
p349 http://www.dailycelebrations.com/112999.htm
p370 http://www.boxing-memorabilia.com/Muhammad_Ali_Quotes_2.htm
p372 http://quotations.home.worldnet.att.net/ muhammadali.html
p379 David Josar, "Ali is in Granholm's corner," *Detroit News,* October 2006

CHAPTER 7

p392 http://news.minnesota.publicradio.org/features/2006/01/31_ap_corettaking/
p396 "Laila Ali says her dad's disease getting worse" by Steve Springer, *Los Angeles Times,* Sunday, October 30, 2005
p399 http://www.cbsnews.com/ stories/1999/02/04/archive/main31586.shtml

Selected Bibliography

There are hundreds of books written about Muhammad Ali but there are only a few that to my mind are indispensable: and without which my own perspective on Ali would be sorely lacking.

They are:

The Lost Legacy of Muhammad Ali Thomas Hauser (Hardcover, 2005)
Muhammad Ali: His Life and Times Thomas Hauser (Paperback, 1992)
The Soul of a Butterfly: Reflections on Life's Journey Muhammad Ali and Hana Yasmeen Ali (Hardcover, 2004)
Redemption Song: Muhammad Ali and the Spirit of the Sixties Mike Marqusee (Paperback, 2005)
King of the World: Muhammed Ali and the Rise of an American Hero David Remnick (Paperback, 1999)
Sound and Fury: Two Powerful Lives, One Fateful Friendship Dave Kindred (Hardcover, 2006)
Sportsworld: An American Dreamland Robert Lipsyte (Paperback, 1977). This book covers a variety of sports and personalities but the section on Ali is the best.
On Boxing Joyce Carol Oates (Paperback, 1997)

There are also two documentaries that capture both the politics of the day and Ali's place within them. They are:

When We Were Kings Leon Gast
Muhammad Ali: Through The Eyes of the World Phil Grabsky

further reading

The Greatest: Muhammad Ali Walter Dean Myers (Paperback, 2001)

Muhammad Ali Memories photographs by Neil Leifer, text by Thomas Hauser (Hardcover, 1992)

The Muhammad Ali Reader edited by Gerald Early (Paperback, 2001)

Muhammad Ali: the Eyewitness Story of a Boxing Legend Alan Goldstein Hardcover, 2002)

The Tao of Muhammad Ali Davis Miller (Paperback, 1992)

Muhammad Ali Greatest of All Time Robert Cassidy (Paperback, 1999)

Muhammad Ali: A View From the Corner Ferdie Pacheco (Hardcover, 1992)

Voices from the Plain of Jars Fred Branfman (Hardcover, 1972)

Born on the Fourth of July Ron Kovic (Updated paperback, 2005)

The Vietnam War and American Culture eds, John Carlos Rowe and Rick Berg (Hardcover, 1991)

A Student Generation in Revolt Ronald Fraser (Paperback, 1988)

An Original Man: The Life and Times of Elijah Muhammad Claude Andrew Clegg (Paperback, 1997)

The Autobiography W.E.B., Du Bois (Paperback, 1968)

King, Martin Luther, Jr., A Testament of Hope: Essential Writings and Speeches ed. James M. Washington (Paperback, 1990)

The Autobiography of Malcolm X Malcolm X, with the assistance of Alex Haley (Paperback, 2001)

You Send Me: The Life and Times of Sam Cooke Daniel Wolff (Paperback, 1996)

Muhammad Ali's Fight Record

Heavyweight Champion 1964–67, 1974–78, 1978–79

Total fights: 61   KO: 37   W: 19   L: 4   KO'd: 1

KEY:
W = Won by decision; L = Lost by decision; KO = Knock out;
KO'd = Knocked out; TKO = Technical knock out; WORLD:
World Heavyweight Championship

1960
Oct 29 Tunney Hunsaker, Louisville Kentucky, W6
Dec 27 Herb Siler, Miami Beach, Florida, KO4

1961
Jan 17 Anthony Sperti, Miami Beach, Florida, KO3
Feb 7   Jim Robinson, Miami Beach, Florida, KO1
Feb 21 Donnie Fleeman, Miami Beach, Florida, KO7
Apr 19 Lamar Clark, Louisville, Kentucky, KO2
June 26 Duke Sabedong, Las Vegas, Nevada W10
July 22 Alonzo Johnson, Louisville, Kentucky, W10
Oct 7 Alex Miteff, Louisville, Kentucky, KO6
Nov 29 Willie Besmanoff, Louisville, Kentucky, KO7

1962
Feb 10 Sonny Banks, New York, New York, KO4

Feb 28 Don Warner, Miami Beach, Florida KO4
Apr 23 George Logan, Los Angeles, California, KO6
May 19 Billy Daniels, New York, New York, KO7
July 20 Alejandro Lavorante, Los Angeles, California, KO5
Nov 15 Archie Moore, Los Angeles, California, KO4

1963
Jan 24 Charlie Powell, Pittsburgh, Pennsylvania, KO3
Mar 13 Doug Jones, New York, New York, W10
June 18 Henry Cooper, London, England, KO5

1964
Feb 25 Sonny Liston, Miami Beach, Florida, TKO7, WORLD

1965
May 25 Sonny Liston, Lewiston, Maine, KO1, WORLD
Nov 22 Floyd Patterson, Las Vegas, Nevada KO12, WORLD

1966
Mar 29 George Chuvalo, Toronto, Canada, W15, WORLD
May 21 Henry Cooper, London, England, KO6, WORLD
Aug 6   Brian London, London, England, KO3, WORLD
Sept 10 Karl Mildenberger, Frankfurt, Germany, KO12, WORLD
Nov 14 Cleveland Williams, Houston, Texas, KO3, WORLD

1967
Feb 6   Ernie Terrell, Houston, Texas, W15, WORLD
Mar 22 Zora Folley, New York, New York, KO7, WORLD

1970

Oct 26 Jerry Quarry, Atlanta, Georgia, KO3

Dec 7   Oscar Bonavena, New York, New York, KO15

1971

Mar 8   Joe Frazier, New York, New York, L15, WORLD

July 26 Jimmy Ellis, Houston, Texas, KO12

Nov 17 Buster Mathis, Houston, Texas, W12

Dec 26 Jurgen Blin, Zurich, Switzerland, KO7

1972

Apr 1   Mac Foster, Tokyo, Japan, W15

May 1   George Chuvalo, Vancouver, Canada, W12

June 27 Jerry Quarry, Las Vegas, Nevada, KO7

July 19 Alvin Lewis, Dublin, Ireland, KO11

Sept 20 Floyd Patterson, New York, New York, KO8

Nov 21 Bob Foster, Stateline, Nevada KO8

1973

Feb 14 Joe Bugner, Las Vegas, Nevada, W12

Mar 31 Ken Norton, San Diego, California, L12

Sept 10 Ken Norton, Los Angeles, California, W12

Oct 20   Rudy Lubbers, Jakarta, Indonesia, W12

1974

Jan 28 Joe Frazier, New York, New York, W12

Oct 30 George Foreman, Kinshasa, Zaire, KO8, WORLD

975

Mar 24 Chuck Wepner, Cleveland, Ohio, KO15, WORLD

May 16 Ron Lyle, Las Vegas, Nevada, KO11, WORLD

June 30 Joe Bugner, Kuala Lumpur, Malaysia, W15, WORLD

Oct 1 Joe Frazier, Quezon City, Philippines, KO14, WORLD

1976

Feb 20 Jean-Pierre Coopman, Hato Rey, Puerto Rico, KO5, WORLD

Apr 30 Jimmy Young, Landover, Maryland, W15, WORLD

May 24 Richard Dunn, Munich, Germany, KO5, WORLD

Sept 28 Ken Norton, New York, New York, W15, WORLD

1977

May 16 Alfredo Evangelista, Landover, Maryland, W15, WORLD

Sept 29 Earnie Shavers, New York, New York, W15, WORLD

1978

Feb 15 Leon Spinks, Las Vegas, Nevada, L15, WORLD

Sept 15 Leon Spinks, New Orleans, Louisiana, W15, WORLD

1980

Oct 2 Larry Holmes, Las Vegas, Nevada, KO'd 11, WORLD

1981

Dec 11 Trevor Berbick, Nassau, Bahamas, L10

Acknowledgments

Initial thanks must go first and foremost to Muhammad Ali for daring to be beyond great. No athlete has ever fed starving sports writers with more material, and no public figure has ever come closer to matching his words with deeds.

But for all of Ali's accomplishments, he didn't put together this book. That credit goes to the talented, creative team at MQ Publications. Any book worth a damn is a collaborative effort and this one is no exception. Specific recognition must go to editors Yvonne Deutch and Gareth Jenkins for nurturing this work to completion. And thanks to my friend and comrade Anthony Arnove for connecting me with the people at MQ.

There are four writers that helped me forge a framework for understanding the elusive Ali: Robert Lipsyte, Mike Marqusee and Thomas Hauser who were both generous with their time and (tried) to keep me from being too starry-eyed about my subject. The parts of this book I am proudest of flow from their influence. And to *Subterranean Fire* author Sharon Smith: the first person to encourage me to read, write, and generalize about this rich subject.

Praise to everyone who taught me that sports and politics could dance together in dynamic fashion. Special thanks to Eddie Mustafa Muhammad. And thank you Dave Meggyesy, Jim Bouton, Billie Jean King, Dr. Harry Edwards, John Carlos, Jim Brown, Marvin Miller, Etan Thomas, and the 1986 Mets.

Lastly to family: To Michele who bought me my first Ali book. You—need I say it?—are the greatest. Thanks to my incredibly supportive in-laws: the Bollinger, Stephan, Fouse crew: Ed, Susan, Meme, Pop-Pop. Bryan, Denise and Matt. To Marlene (Gramaleni), Peter, Maggie and Mike for being a part of my family. And to Annie, Jason, and Amira for being true to the game. And lastly to my soon-to-be three-year-old Sasha Jane, who floats like a butterfly and has started to sting like a bee. I couldn't be prouder.

Dedication

To my mother Jane Zirin who taught me from day one to ask questions of the world … always had time to toss the football, throw a baseball, and even box.

To my father Jim Zirin who introduced me to Ali without prejudice and—not unlike Angelo Dundee—has always been in my corner.

Index

Page numbers in *italics* refer to captions

First published by MQ Publications Ltd
12 The Ivories
6–8 Northampton Street
London, N1 2HY
Tel: 020 7359 2244
Fax: 020 7359 1616
email: mail@mqpublications.com
website: www.mqpublications.com

North American Office:
49 West 24th Street, 8th Floor
New York, NY 10010
email: information@mqpublicationsus.com

MQP Handbooks Director: Gareth Jenkins
MQP Handbooks Series Editor: Yvonne Deutch

ISBN: 978-1-84072-684-8

10 9 8 7 6 5 4 3 2 1

Printed in China

★ 1971

Mar 8 — Incensed at Ali calling him an "Uncle Tom", Joe Frazier inflicts first defeat on Ali on points, at Madison Square Garden. They split a $5 million purse

Jun 28 — Supreme Court unanimously overturns his draft conviction

Jul 26 — Defeats former sparring partner Jimmy Ellis in a 12-round technical knockout

★ 1972

Jul 19 — Knocks out Al Lewis in 11th round

Sep 20 — Knocks out Floyd Patterson in 7th round

★ 1973

Mar 31 — Fights 10 rounds with a broken jaw before losing a 12-round decision to Ken Norton

Sep 10 — Wins rematch with Ken Norton

★ 1974

Jan 28 — Wins 12-round decision over Joe Frazier, who has lost his title to George Foreman

Oct 30 — Fights George Foreman in Zaire, splitting a $10 million purse, and scores an 8th-round knockout

★ 1975

Elijah Muhammad dies and is succeeded as head of the Nation of Islam by his son Wallace. Ali converts to orthodox Sunni Islam

Mar 24 — Knocks out Chuck Wepner in the 15th round in Cleveland, a fight that inspired the movie "Rocky" with Sylvester Stallone

Jun 30 — Defeats Joe Bugner on points

Oct 1 — Ali defeats Joe Frazier in Manila in rounds in perhaps the most brutal b match ever

★ 1976

Pays $400,000 for a farm in Berrie Springs, Michigan

Sep 28 — Defeats Ken Norton on points

★ 1977

Jan — Divorces Khalilah in a $2 million sett

Jun — Marries model Veronica Porche. They two daughters, Laila (who becomes a professional boxer) and Hana

May 16 — Defeats Alfredo Evangelista on points

Sep 29 — Defeats Earnie Shavers on points

★ 1978

Feb 15 — Loses title to Leon Spinks in Las Veg a 15 round split decision

Aug 15 — Regains title from Leon Spinks in New Orleans in a 15 round split decision, becoming the first boxer to win the heavyweight title three times

Louisville's Walnut Street, where Ali gr renamed Muhammad Ali Boulevard

★ 1979

Jun 27 — Announces retirement and vacates the

★ 1980

Oct 2 — Challenges former sparring partner Lar Holmes for the WBC world heavyweigh in Las Vegas. Suffers a technical knock in the 11th round—the first time in 6C professional bouts he fails to go the distance